hamlyn
QuickCook

hamlyn

QuickCook
Moroccan

Recipes by Ghillie Basan

Every dish, three ways – you choose!
30 minutes | 20 minutes | 10 minutes

An Hachette UK Company
www.hachette.co.uk

First published in Great Britain in 2013 by Hamlyn,
a division of Octopus Publishing Group Ltd
Endeavour House, 189 Shaftesbury Avenue
London WC2H 8JY
www.octopusbooks.co.uk

ISBN 978-0-600-62581-0

A CIP catalogue record for this book is available from the British Library

Printed and bound in China

10 9 8 7 6 5 4 3 2 1

Both metric and imperial measurements are given for the recipes. Use one set of
measures only, not a mixture of both.

Standard level spoon measurements are used in all recipes
1 tablespoon = 15 ml
1 teaspoon = 5 ml

Ovens should be preheated to the specified temperature. If using a fan-assisted oven,
follow the manufacturer's instructions for adjusting the time and temperature. Grills
should also be preheated.

This book includes dishes made with nuts and nut derivatives. It is advisable for
those with known allergic reactions to nuts and nut derivatives and those who may
be potentially vulnerable to these allergies, such as pregnant and nursing mothers,
invalids, the elderly, babies and children, to avoid dishes made with nuts and nut oils.

It is also prudent to check the labels of preprepared ingredients for the possible
inclusion of nut derivatives.

The Department of Health advises that eggs should not be consumed raw. This book
contains some dishes made with raw or lightly cooked eggs. It is prudent for more
vulnerable people such as pregnant and nursing mothers, invalids, the elderly, babies
and young children to avoid uncooked or lightly cooked dishes made with eggs.

Contents

Introduction

30 20 10 – Quick, Quicker, Quickest

This book offers a new and flexible approach to
meal-planning for busy cooks, letting you choose the
recipe option that best fits the time you have available.
Inside you will find 360 dishes that will inspire and
motivate you to get cooking every day of the year.
All the recipes take a maximum of 30 minutes to cook.
Some take as little as 20 minutes and, amazingly, many
take only 10 minutes. With a bit of preparation, you can
easily try out one new recipe from this book each night
and slowly you will be able to build a wide and exciting
portfolio of recipes to suit your needs.

How Does it Work?

Every recipe in the QuickCook series can be cooked one
of three ways – a 30-minute version, a 20-minute
version or a super-quick and easy 10-minute version.
At the beginning of each chapter you'll find recipes
listed by time. Choose a dish based on how much time
you have and turn to that page.

You'll find the main recipe in the middle of the page
accompanied by a beautiful photograph, as well as two
time-variation recipes below.

If you enjoy your chosen dish, why not go back and cook the other time-variation options at a later date? So, if you liked the 20-minute Roasted Chilli and Preserved Lemon Sardines, but only have 10 minutes to spare this time around, you'll find a way to cook it using cheat ingredients or clever shortcuts.

If you love the ingredients and flavours of the 10-minute Simple Fresh Fruit Kebabs, why not try something more substantial like the 20-minute Chilled Rosewater Fruit Salad, or be inspired to make a more elaborate version, like the Poached Red Wine and Rosewater Fruit? Alternatively, browse through all 360 delicious recipes, find something that catches your eye – then cook the version that fits your time-frame.

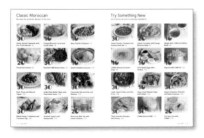

Or, for easy inspiration, turn to the gallery on pages 12–19 to get an instant overview by themes, such as Classic Moroccan or Try Something New.

QuickCook Online

To make life easier, you can use the special code on each recipe page to email yourself a recipe card for printing, or email a text-only shopping list to your phone. Go to www.hamlynquickcook.com and enter the recipe code at the bottom of each page.

 MOR-GRIL-NOQ

QuickCook Moroccan

Moroccan food is truly a feast for the senses – fragrant, fiery, sweet and salty. Fruity, syrupy tagines, buttery couscous with scented broths, crispy pastries, tangy salads and spicy sauces, this is a cuisine that reflects a colourful history of different peoples and their culinary cultures.

Geographically, perched at the north-west corner of the African continent, Morocco acts as a culinary gateway to the native influences of central and northern Africa, to the ancient and medieval traditions of the Arab world to the east, and to the Andalusian flavours of southern Spain across the water. When the Arabs took over the region between the 7th and 14th centuries, they brought spices, nuts and dried fruits and they also brought Islam and its dietary restrictions. When the Moors were expelled from Spain they returned with olives, olive oil, tomatoes and paprika, while the the Jewish refugees fleeing the Spanish Inquisition brought their valuable preserving techniques, such as the ubiquitous preserved lemons. The French, who colonized parts of Morocco, also left their stamp on the cooking as well as wine-making and their language.

Rich in culture and produce, Morocco weaves the medieval with the modern, from the mountain-top villages to the majestic cities of ancient dynasties and from the deserts with their date-palm oases to the coastline fringed with sun-drenched tourist beaches. This is true of the culinary culture too – medieval recipes with modern twists, a unique blend of the sensual and the exotic.

Traditions of Moroccan Food

The influence of Islam on Morocco's population does have an effect on the method of killing and preparation of meat (Muslims don't eat pork) and the consumption of alcoholic beverages. However, Morocco is home to a variety of religions and tribal people and does produce its own wines and aperitifs. Morocco is famous for its steaming glasses of sweet mint tea, which is offered as a traditional mark of hospitality. The tea itself is simple to make but the ceremony surrounding it is important. It is presented in an elaborate teapot, which is held high to pour the steaming amber liquid into glasses so that a little foam forms on the surface, and milk is never added.

Coffee, on the other hand, is more of a café beverage, or reserved for special occasions, and it is usually served black, spiked with aromatic cardamom seeds or cinnamon sticks, in small cups.

The souks and the old medinas are the lungs of Morocco's culinary culture. Magical and enticing, filled with arresting aromas and colourful displays, they are bustling venues for haggling, meal planning and snacking. Everything you need to make a meal is available in the street markets: dried apricots, dates, prunes and figs; roasted almonds, walnuts and pistachios; big bunches of flat leaf parsley, mint and coriander; tubs of spices and dried herbs; vats of olives, bottles of oils and jars of pickles and preserves; the distilled waters of rose petals and orange blossom; sacks of flour, grains and couscous; earthenware tagines with their conical lids; and large copper k'dras for celebratory feasts.

A predominant feature of Moroccan cooking, a tagine is essentially a glorified slow-cooked stew, deeply aromatic and full of flavour. The word 'tagine' is both the name of the cooked dish and of the cooking vessel. Placed over a charcoal stove, which disperses the heat all around the base, a tagine enables the ingredients to cook gently in the steam, which builds up inside the lid, so that they remain tender and moist. Generally a tagine is served from the cooking vessel with bread to mop up all the delectable juices, or with couscous.

The word 'couscous' refers to the granules as well as the cooked dish, which is traditionally prepared in a 'couscoussier' – a two-tiered pot with a stewing section at the base for the meat, beans or vegetables, and a steaming pot on top for the couscous. Couscous is Morocco's national dish and the preparation of it is such an important part of the culinary life that it determines the status of a cook's ability. Although referred to as a 'grain' it is not technically one; instead it could be described as Moroccan 'pasta' as it is made with semolina flour, which is mixed with water and hand-rolled to different sizes.

For the recipes in *QuickCook Moroccan* the shop-bought couscous granules have already been steamed and dried so they can be prepared quickly; the tagines have been adapted to suit quicker cooking times; and some traditional pickle and preserve recipes have been included as they play a key role in Moroccan cuisine – it is important to note that the method is quick but time for preserving is required, although many are available pre-prepared.

A Moroccan Meal

Family and food play a big role in Moroccan life and there are many religious and celebratory occasions for festive feasts. Most Moroccan meals begin with a selection of little dishes, ranging from a simple bowl of marinated olives to puréed vegetable dips, savoury pastries and tangy fruit and vegetable salads, which are served to whet the appetite. A bowl of soup or a tagine might follow, served with a mound of couscous or freshly baked bread. Alternatively, the couscous may be served as a course on its own. Grilled or roasted meat, chicken or fish might follow and fresh fruit usually completes the meal. On special occasions, the meal will end with a dessert, but most sweet dishes are enjoyed on their own at different times of the day, or they are served as offerings of hospitality and reserved for celebratory feasts. Once the meal is over, glasses of steaming mint tea will be served to aid digestion.

QuickCook Ingredients

Argan oil: Dark in colour with a reddish tinge and nutty flavour, this is the main cooking oil of the southern region of Morocco where the stout, thorny argan trees grow. The goats climb the trees and eat the fleshy exterior of the fruit, which resemble large green olives, and then excrete the nut. The herders or village women collect the nuts and crack them open to extract the kernels, which are then roasted and ground to extract the oil.

Bread: In general, bread is made daily in traditional community ovens and, in rural communities, it is served with every meal to act as a scoop and as a mop to soak up all the delectable sauces. There are a variety of Moroccan breads but the most common are flatbreads, semolina buns and baguette-style loaves.

Chermoula: Prepared predominantly with chillies, garlic, cumin seeds, lemon juice and fresh coriander, chermoula is used as a marinade or sauce for grilled fish and poultry dishes, and some tagines. Quantities and ingredients vary from region to region.

Dukkah: Originally from Egypt, this coarsely ground nut, seed and spice mix is often combined with oil to form a dip for bread or vegetables. The basic mix consists of roasted hazelnuts, sesame seeds and roasted cumin and coriander seeds. Dried chillies, paprika, dried mint and dried thyme are often added too.

Harissa: Prepared by pounding dried red chillies that have been soaked in water, or chillies roasted in oil, with spices and fresh coriander, harissa is a fiery paste. It is served as a condiment to accompany meat, fish and vegetable dishes; it is added to marinades and sauces; and it is blended with yogurt or olive oil to make a delicious dip.

Preserved lemons: The small, native, thin-skinned lemons are preserved in salt and lemon juice and only the finely chopped or sliced rind is used for cooking and garnishing to impart a distinctive citrus flavour to tagines, grilled dishes and salads.

Ras el hanout: Translated from Arabic as 'head of the shop' this is a delightful medley of 30–40 different spices, some of which are indigenous to the region. Beyond the souks of Morocco, it is difficult to make an authentic ras el hanout, but you can create your own versions by grinding together equal quantities of peppercorns, cloves, nigella seeds, allspice berries, mace, coriander seeds and cumin seeds and then adding ground ginger, ground cinnamon, dried lavender and dried rose petals.

Smen: An acquired taste, smen is an aged butter with a rancid flavour. Set in earthenware pots and stored in a cool, dry place for months, it is regarded as an essential component in some tagines. A good substitute is ghee, which is clarified butter and, although it has a warm aroma and a nutty flavour rather than the pungent one of smen, it gives the same kind of depth to a dish.

Tabil: This is a North African spice mix that is often used to flavour grilled dishes and street food. To make your own, grind equal quantities of coriander seeds, caraway seeds, dried chilli and salt, to which you can add roasted crushed garlic and roasted chickpeas and sesame seeds.

Zahtar: Originally from the Middle East, this is a popular street spice used for sprinkling over grilled and fried food and savoury pastries. To make your own, combine equal quantities of roasted sesame seeds and dried thyme with sumac and a little sea salt.

Classic Moroccan

Recreate the authentic flavours of the souk.

Herby Spinach Tapenade with
Pan-Fried Haloumi 30

Orange Blossom Carrot and
Cumin Salad 34

Spicy Paprika Chickpeas 52

Preserved Lemons 68

Roasted Chilli Harissa Paste 70

Quick Cinnamon Couscous 128

Beef, Prune and Almond
Tagine 150

Grilled Red Mullet Fillets with
Chermoula Sauce 200

Chermoula Fish and Vine Leaf
Skewers 214

Baked Honey, Cardamom and
Cinnamon Figs 246

Strained Yogurt with
Honeycomb 270

Moroccan Mint Tea with
Lemon Verbena 274

Try Something New

Add a Moroccan twist to everyday ingredients.

Sweet Tomato, Cinnamon and Sesame Seed Jam 32

Sweet Cucumber and Orange Blossom Salad 42

Simple Herb, Chilli and Saffron Broth 90

Chilled Almond and Garlic Soup 94

Soft-Boiled Eggs with Harissa 114

Popcorn with Chilli Oil 120

Lamb, Sweet Potato and Okra K'dra 148

Deep-Fried Plantain Chips with Zahtar 226

Sweet Cinnamon, Pistachio and Raisin Couscous 240

Thick Semolina Pancakes with Honey 256

Chilled Almond Milk 272

Hot Spicy Tea with Chillies 276

Chicken and Poultry

Satisfying suppers infused with warm and aromatic flavours.

Honeyed Pumpkin and Ginger Broth 78

Minty Chicken and Rice Soup 88

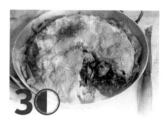

Chicken, Nut and Cinnamon Pie 100

Chicken, Green Olive and Preserved Lemon Tagine 144

Cinnamon Duck and Caramelized Pear Tagine 158

Herby Carrot, Potato and Pea Tagine 164

Saffron, Onion, Chicken, Turnip and Chickpea K'dra 174

Roasted Cinnamon Chicken Thighs and Plums 190

Roasted Honeyed Quince and Duck Legs 192

Pan-Fried Quails with Ginger and Grapes 194

Chargrilled Harissa Chicken Wings with Burnt Oranges 196

Chicken Livers and Pomegranate Syrup on Fried Bread 198

Meaty Treats

Hearty dishes to warm your soul.

Lamb, Chickpea and Cinnamon Broth 80

Lemony Beef, Bean and Cumin Soup 82

Mini Lamb and Harissa Pizzas 106

Chorizo and Parsley Eggs 108

Couscous Tfaia with Beef 132

Cardamom Lamb and Dates 160

Chorizo, Lentil and Fenugreek Tagine 162

Moroccan Onion and Lamb Kebabs 180

Moroccan Onion and Cumin Beef Burgers 182

Fennel-Roasted Lamb Fillet with Honeyed Figs 184

Spicy Chargrilled Meatballs with Toasted Coconut 186

Spicy Pan-Fried Liver, Prunes and Onions 188

Veggie Delights

A feast of flavours to add colour to your table.

Onion, Parsley, Tomato and
Pomegranate Syrup Salad 36

Herby Tomato, Caper and
Preserved Lemon Salad 40

Warm Garlicky Lentil Salad 50

Tomato, Ras el Hanout
and Vermicelli Soup 76

Carrot, Coriander
and Lentil Soup 92

Courgette, Mint and
Bread Omelette 110

Chilli and Herb Sweet
Potato Pancakes 112

Couscous with Spring
Vegetables and Dill 134

Three Pepper, Olive, Feta
and Egg Tagine 166

Ras el Hanout Lentils
and Chickpeas 172

Vegetable Kebabs with
Harissa Yogurt 216

Roasted Spiced Pumpkin 224

Fish and Seafood

Spicy seafood to turn up the heat.

Fino, Harissa and Grilled Pepper Fish Soup 84

Mussel, Chilli and Coriander Broth 86

Deep-Fried Fish and Chermoula Pastries 104

Lemon Couscous with Spicy Shellfish 138

Chermoula Monkfish and Black Olive Tagine 146

Toasted Saffron, Herb and Preserved Lemon Fish Tagine 154

Herby Prawn, Tomato and Turmeric Fennel Tagine 156

Seared Harissa Tuna Steaks 204

Swordfish, Bay and Lime Kebabs 206

Griddled Turmeric Squid with Crushed Chickpeas 208

Chargrilled Chilli Prawns with Lime 210

Mini Saffron Fish Balls 212

Fruity Dishes

Tempting dishes bursting with fragrance.

Olive, Caper and Bitter
Orange Relish 24

Pink Grapefruit and Fennel
Salad 38

Artichoke, Clementine and
Preserved Lemon Salad 46

Beetroot, Apple and Orange
Blossom Salad 48

Apple and Butternut Soup
with Chilli Oil 96

Chilli, Lime and Coriander
Dried Fruit and Nuts 116

Spicy Pine Nut and Apricot
Couscous 130

Ginger and Honey Lamb
and Apricot Tagine 140

Spicy Courgette, Aubergine
and Date Tagine 168

Watermelon, Rosewater
and Lemon Balm Salad 232

Hot Spiced Dried Fruit
Compote 250

Simple Fresh Fruit Kebabs 252

Great for Entertaining

Indulgent dishes designed to impress.

Pear, Chicory and Rose Petal Salad 60

Chilli and Fino Gazpacho 98

Parsnip and Beetroot Crisps with Homemade Dukkah 118

Cheese and Paprika Potato Cakes 122

Couscous with Orangey Fennel and Courgette 136

Spicy Beef, Sun-Dried Tomatoes and Pine Nuts 142

Roasted Chilli and Preserved Lemon Sardines 202

Roasted Coriander and Preserved Lemon Potatoes 222

Date and Pistachio Truffles 238

Crystallized Rose Petals 258

Saffron Pears with Honey and Lavender 264

Moroccan Coffee with Cardamom 278

QuickCook

Starters, Salads, Pickles and Preserves

Recipes listed by cooking time

30

20

10

20 Olive, Caper and Bitter Orange Relish

Serves 4

2 tomatoes

150 g (5 oz) fleshy black olives, pitted and roughly chopped

finely chopped rind of 1 small fresh or preserved bitter orange

2 garlic cloves, crushed

1 scant teaspoon ground cumin

1 tablespoon baby capers, rinsed and drained

1 tablespoon olive oil

salt and pepper

toasted flatbreads, to serve (optional)

- Place the tomatoes in a heatproof bowl and pour over boiling water to cover. Leave for 1–2 minutes, then drain, cut a cross at the stem end of each tomato and peel off the skins. Cut into quarters, remove the seeds and roughly chop the flesh.

- Put the chopped tomatoes and olives into a bowl. Add the orange rind, garlic and cumin and season. Stir in the capers, then add the oil and mix well. Leave to stand for at least 10 minutes before serving, with toasted flatbreads, if liked.

 Orangey Spiced Olives

Put 350 g (11½ oz) rinsed and drained cracked green olives into a bowl. Dry-fry 1 teaspoon each of cumin seeds, coriander seeds and cardamom seeds and ½ teaspoon black peppercorns in a small, heavy-based frying pan for 1–2 minutes over a medium heat until they emit a nutty aroma. Using a pestle and mortar, crush the spices, then add to the olives with 2–3 tablespoons olive oil, the juice of 1 orange and 1–2 teaspoons harissa paste (see page 70). Mix well and serve. (The olives can also be stored in a sealed sterilized jar in the refrigerator for up to 2 weeks.)

 Olive, Feta and Bitter Orange Salad

Using a sharp knife, pit 450 g (14½ oz) fleshy green olives and cut into slivers, then tip into a bowl. Dry-fry 2 teaspoons coriander seeds in a small, heavy-based frying pan over a medium heat for 2 minutes until they emit a nutty aroma. Using a pestle and mortar, crush the seeds, then add to the olives with the finely sliced rind of 1 fresh or preserved bitter orange. Toss with 2 tablespoons olive oil and 1 tablespoon balsamic vinegar, then leave to stand for at least 10 minutes to let the flavours mingle. Scatter over 100 g (3½ oz) crumbled feta cheese and serve with chunks of warm crusty bread.

 # Harissa Aubergines with Goats' Cheese Toasts

Serves 4

2–3 tablespoons olive or argan oil

1 aubergine, diced

2 teaspoons harissa paste
(see page 70)

1–2 tablespoons water

1 teaspoon sugar

1 tablespoon finely chopped
flat leaf parsley

salt and pepper

To serve

creamy or crumbly goats' cheese

toasted flatbreads

- Heat the oil in a heavy-based frying pan, stir in the aubergine and cook for 2–3 minutes until lightly browned. Stir in the harissa and mix well.

- Add the measurement water and sugar and cook for a further 2–3 minutes. Season and sprinkle with the parsley. Serve with creamy or crumbly goats' cheese on toasted flatbreads.

 ### Smoked Aubergine and Harissa Dip

Place 2 aubergines over a gas flame, smoke and cook for 10–12 minutes, turning occasionally until the skin begins to char and flake – it may even burst in places. When soft, place in a plastic food bag to sweat for 2–3 minutes. Hold by the stalks under cold running water and gently peel off the skin. Squeeze out any excess water and place on a board. Remove the stalks, then chop the flesh to a pulp and tip into a bowl. Add 3–4 tablespoons thick natural yogurt, 2 teaspoons harissa paste (see page 70) and 1–2 tablespoons finely chopped coriander. Season and mix well. Serve with crusty bread.

 ### Aubergine, Harissa and Tomato Dip

Place 2 peeled and cubed aubergines in a steamer and steam for 8–10 minutes until soft. Tip onto a board and mash with a fork. Heat 2–3 tablespoons olive oil in a heavy-based saucepan, stir in 1–2 teaspoons cumin seeds and 2–3 crushed garlic cloves and cook until fragrant. Add a 400 g (13 oz) can chopped tomatoes, drained of juice, 1–2 teaspoons each of sugar and harissa paste (see page 70) and 2 tablespoons finely chopped flat leaf parsley and cook over a low heat for 10–15 minutes until thickened. Stir in the juice of 1 lemon and the mashed aubergines, mix well and heat through. Season to taste. Garnish with a little more finely chopped parsley and serve warm or at room temperature with chunks of crusty bread.

MOR-STAR-DEV

Broad Bean Dip with Preserved Lemon

Serves 4

700–900 g (1½–2lb) fresh
   broad beans, podded
2–3 garlic cloves, halved
1–2 teaspoons ground cumin
1 teaspoon ground coriander
3 tablespoons olive oil
juice of ½ lemon
1–2 teaspoons finely chopped
   preserved lemon rind
   (see page 68)
salt and pepper
toasted flatbreads or crudités,
   to serve

- Cook the beans in a saucepan of boiling water for 3–4 minutes until tender. Drain, then pop the larger beans out of their tough skins (the smaller beans don't need to be skinned).

- Using a large pestle and mortar, pound the beans, garlic and ground spices to a smooth paste. Alternatively, whizz in a food processor. Gradually mix in the oil and lemon juice to form a smooth purée, then season well.

- Tip the purée into a serving bowl and sprinkle over the preserved lemon rind. Serve warm or at room temperature with toasted flatbreads or crudités.

Broad Bean, Preserved Lemon and Mint Salad Cook 700 g (1½ lb) podded fresh or frozen broad beans in a saucepan of boiling water for 3–4 minutes until tender. Drain and refresh under cold running water, then pop the beans out of their tough skins. Tip the beans into a bowl and toss with 2 tablespoons olive oil and 1 tablespoon balsamic vinegar. Add 1–2 teaspoons finely sliced preserved lemon rind (see page 68) and a finely shredded small bunch of mint leaves. Season well and serve.

Broad Bean, Carrot, Preserved Lemon and Egg Salad Cook 450 g (14½ oz) podded fresh or frozen broad beans in a saucepan of boiling water for 3–4 minutes until tender. Drain and refresh under cold running water, then pop the larger beans out of their skins and set all the beans aside. Steam 2–3 peeled and sliced carrots for 5 minutes, or until tender but not soft. Drain and refresh under cold running water. Place the beans, carrots and 1 red onion, cut into bite-sized pieces, in a bowl and add the finely sliced rind of 1 preserved lemon (see page 68) and a roughly chopped small bunch of flat leaf parsley. Mix together 2 tablespoons olive or argan oil, the juice of 1 lemon, 2 crushed garlic cloves and 1 teaspoon crushed cumin seeds and season. Pour over the salad and toss well, then spoon onto a serving dish. Cook 3–4 eggs in a saucepan of boiling water for about 4 minutes, then drain and shell. Cut into quarters and arrange on the salad. Sprinkle over a little paprika and serve while the eggs are still warm.

30 Herby Spinach Tapenade with Pan-Fried Haloumi

Serves 4

225 g (7½ oz) baby spinach leaves

handful of celery leaves

2 tablespoons olive oil

2–3 garlic cloves, crushed

1 teaspoon cumin seeds

6–8 black olives, pitted and
finely chopped

large bunch of flat leaf parsley,
finely chopped

large bunch of coriander,
finely chopped

1 teaspoon Spanish smoked paprika

juice of ½ lemon

salt and pepper

For the haloumi

2 tablespoons olive oil

225 g (7½ oz) haloumi cheese,
sliced

- Place the spinach and celery leaves in a steamer and cook for 10–15 minutes until soft. Refresh under cold running water, then drain well and squeeze out the excess water. Chop to a fine pulp.

- Heat the oil in a heavy-based frying pan, stir in the garlic and cumin seeds and cook until they emit a nutty aroma. Stir in the olives, parsley, coriander and paprika. Add the spinach and celery leaves, season well and cook gently for 8–10 minutes until the mixture is smooth.

- Meanwhile, cook the haloumi. Heat the oil in a separate heavy-based frying pan, add the haloumi and fry for 3–4 minutes, turning once, until golden brown and crispy. Drain on kitchen paper.

- Tip the spinach mixture into a bowl, add the lemon juice and mix well. Serve warm with the fried haloumi.

Spinach and Herb Yogurt

Steam 225 g (7½ oz) baby spinach leaves with a small bunch each of flat leaf parsley and mint leaves for about 8 minutes, or until soft. Meanwhile, beat together 250 g (8 oz) thick natural yogurt, 2 crushed garlic cloves and 1 scant teaspoon ground cumin in a bowl and season well. Squeeze out the excess water from the cooked spinach and herbs, then beat into the yogurt. Serve with chunks of warm crusty bread.

Sautéed Spinach and Herbs

Rinse and drain 150 g (5 oz) spinach leaves, a large bunch of rocket leaves and a large bunch each of flat leaf parsley, mint and coriander, then roughly chop together. Heat 2–3 tablespoons olive oil in a large, heavy-based frying pan, stir in 2 crushed garlic cloves and 1–2 finely chopped green chillies and cook for 1–2 minutes until beginning to colour. Toss in the spinach mixture and cook gently until just wilted. Add the finely chopped rind of ½ preserved lemon (see page 68) and season to taste. Serve warm on toasted bread with dollops of thick natural yogurt.

30 Sweet Tomato, Cinnamon and Sesame Seed Jam

Serves 4

6–8 large ripe tomatoes
2–3 tablespoons olive oil
1 tablespoon tomato purée
2 tablespoons honey
1 teaspoon ground cinnamon
1 teaspoon ground ginger
1 tablespoon sesame seeds
salt and pepper
crusty bread, to serve

- Place the tomatoes in an ovenproof dish, pour over the oil and roast in a preheated oven, 200°C (400°F), Gas Mark 6, for 15 minutes. Remove the tomatoes with a slotted spoon, reserving the oil. Peel off the skins and chop to a pulp.

- Tip the tomatoes into a heavy-based saucepan with the tomato purée and 1 tablespoon of the roasting oil and cook over a high heat until bubbling. Stir in the honey, cinnamon and ginger and cook for a further 5–10 minutes until the mixture is thick, adding more of the oil if necessary.

- Meanwhile, dry-fry the sesame seeds in a small, heavy-based frying pan over a medium heat for 2–3 minutes until golden brown.

- Season the jam, tip it into a serving bowl and sprinkle over the toasted sesame seeds. Serve warm or at room temperature with crusty bread for dipping.

 Spicy Tomato and Sesame Seed Paste Drain and pat dry 200 g (7 oz) sun-dried tomatoes in oil. Using a large pestle and mortar, pound the tomatoes, 2–3 garlic cloves and 1 teaspoon each of ground cumin, ground cinnamon, ground cardamom and harissa paste (see page 70) to a paste. Season with salt and mix with a little olive oil. Alternatively, whizz in a food processor. Spoon into a bowl, scatter over 1–2 teaspoons toasted sesame seeds and serve with chunks of crusty bread.

 Dried Tomato, Feta and Sesame Seed Salad Drain and pat dry 200 g (7 oz) sun-dried tomatoes in oil, then finely slice and place in a bowl. Add 200 g (7 oz) cubed feta cheese and the finely sliced rind of 1 preserved lemon (see page 68). In a separate bowl, mix together 2–3 tablespoons olive or argan oil, the juice of 1 lemon and 1 teaspoon each of crushed coriander seeds, crushed fennel seeds and finely chopped dried red chilli, then pour the dressing over the salad and leave to stand for 5–10 minutes. Serve scattered with 2 teaspoons toasted sesame seeds.

 # Orange Blossom Carrot and Cumin Salad

Serves 4

juice of 1 lemon

2 tablespoons orange blossom water

½ teaspoon ground cumin

1 teaspoon runny honey or sugar

500 g (1 lb) carrots, peeled and grated

salt

ground cinnamon, for dusting

- Mix together the lemon juice, orange blossom water, cumin and honey or sugar in a bowl.

- Place the grated carrots in a serving bowl and pour over the dressing. Season with salt and toss well. Sprinkle over a little cinnamon before serving.

 Warm Carrot and Toasted Cumin Salad Place 450 g (14½ oz) carrots, peeled and cut into sticks, in a steamer and steam for 10–12 minutes until tender but not mushy. Meanwhile, dry-fry 1–2 teaspoons cumin seeds in a small, heavy-based frying pan over a medium heat for 2 minutes until they emit a nutty aroma. Set aside. Tip the carrots into a bowl and, while still warm, toss with 2 tablespoons olive or argan oil, the juice of 1 lemon, 2 crushed garlic cloves, the toasted cumin seeds and 1 teaspoon runny honey. Season well and leave to stand for at least 5 minutes to let the flavours mingle. Just before serving, toss in a finely chopped small bunch each of coriander and mint.

 Herby Roasted Carrot and Cumin Dip Place 500 g (1 lb) carrots, peeled and thickly sliced, in an ovenproof dish and pour over 100 ml (3½ fl oz) olive oil. Place in a preheated oven, 200°C (400°F), Gas Mark 6, for about 15 minutes. Toss with 2 crushed garlic cloves and 2 teaspoons cumin seeds, then return to the oven and cook for a further 10 minutes until the carrots are tender but not soft. Tip into a bowl and crush to a coarse paste using a potato masher. Alternatively, tip into a food processor and whizz to a smooth paste. Mix in the juice of 1 lemon and a finely chopped small bunch each of flat leaf parsley, dill and mint. Season and spoon into a serving bowl. Drizzle over a little olive oil and garnish with extra chopped herbs. Serve warm or at room temperature with strips of toasted flatbread.

Onion, Parsley, Tomato and Pomegranate Syrup Salad

Serves 4

2 tomatoes
large bunch of flat leaf parsley,
    roughly chopped
2 red onions, finely sliced
2 teaspoons coriander seeds
finely sliced rind of 1 preserved
    lemon (see page 68)
2 tablespoons pomegranate syrup
salt and pepper

- Place the tomatoes in a heatproof bowl and pour over boiling water to cover. Leave for 1–2 minutes, then drain, cut a cross at the stem end of each tomato and peel off the skins. Cut into quarters, remove the seeds and roughly chop the flesh. Place in a serving bowl and add the parsley and onions.

- Dry-fry the coriander seeds in a small, heavy-based frying pan over a medium heat for 2 minutes until they emit a nutty aroma. Using a pestle and mortar, lightly crush the seeds. Add to the tomato mixture with the preserved lemon rind. Pour over the pomegranate syrup and season well. Gently toss together and serve.

 Onion, Parsley and Pomegranate Syrup Salad Spread 2 finely sliced white onions on a plate and sprinkle with salt. Leave to stand for 5–8 minutes, then rinse, drain and pat dry. Place in a serving bowl and stir in a chopped small bunch each of flat leaf parsley and mint and 1–2 teaspoons sumac. Drizzle over 1 tablespoon pomegranate syrup and serve.

Parsley, Onion, Walnut, Tomato and Pomegranate Syrup Salad Evenly chop a large bunch of flat leaf parsley, leaves and stalks. Chop 2–3 tablespoons walnuts into bite-sized pieces and place, together with the parsley, in a shallow serving bowl. Add 2–3 tomatoes, skinned and deseeded as above and chopped to the same size as the walnuts, and 1–2 deseeded and finely chopped green chillies, then scatter over 1 finely chopped red onion. Drizzle over 2 tablespoons pomegranate syrup and season well with salt. Leave to stand for 15–20 minutes to allow the onion juices to seep into the salad. Gently toss together and serve with toasted flatbreads.

 # Pink Grapefruit and Fennel Salad

Serves 4

1 fennel bulb
1 tablespoon olive oil
juice of ½ lemon
1 scant teaspoon cumin seeds, crushed
2 pink grapefruit
1 scant teaspoon salt
2–3 spring onions, finely sliced
1 tablespoon black olives, pitted

- Cut the base off the fennel and remove the outer layers. Cut in half lengthways and in half horizontally, then finely slice with the grain. Place in a bowl and toss with the oil, lemon juice and cumin seeds. Leave to marinate for 20 minutes.

- Meanwhile, using a sharp knife, remove the peel and pith from the grapefruit. Holding the grapefruit over a bowl to catch the juice, cut down between the membranes and remove the segments. Cut each segment in half, place in the bowl and sprinkle with the salt. Leave to stand for 5 minutes to draw out the sweet juices.

- Add the fennel to the grapefruit and mix in the spring onions. Serve topped with the olives.

1 Grapefruit and Toasted Fennel Seed Salad

Dry-fry 1–2 teaspoons fennel seeds in a small, heavy-based frying pan over a medium heat for 2 minutes until they emit a nutty aroma, then set aside. Using a sharp knife, remove the peel and pith from 2 sweet grapefruits, then cut down between the membranes and remove the segments. Arrange the segments on a plate and sprinkle with 1 tablespoon orange blossom water. Scatter over the toasted fennel seeds and serve.

2 Orange, Fennel and Apple Salad

Prepare 2 fennel bulbs as above. Place in a bowl and toss with the juice of 1 lemon. Add 2 cored and finely sliced crispy red or green apples and toss to coat well in the lemon juice. Using a sharp knife, remove the peel and pith from 1 orange. Holding the orange over the salad bowl to catch the juice, cut down between the membranes and remove the segments, then add to the bowl. Dry-fry 1–2 tablespoons shelled pistachio nuts in a small, heavy-based frying pan over a medium heat for 1–2 minutes until they begin to colour and emit a nutty aroma. Using a pestle and mortar, pound the pistachios, 1 garlic clove and a small handful of mint leaves to a coarse paste. Mix with 1–2 tablespoons olive oil, then drizzle over the salad. Season and toss well.

Herby Tomato, Caper and Preserved Lemon Salad

Serves 4

4 large tomatoes

finely sliced rind of 1 preserved
   lemon (see page 68)

1 red onion, sliced into
   bite-sized pieces

1–2 tablespoons baby capers,
   rinsed and drained

small bunch of flat leaf parsley,
   finely chopped

small bunch of coriander,
   finely chopped

small bunch of mint,
   finely chopped

2 tablespoons olive or argan oil

juice of ½ lemon

1 scant teaspoon paprika

salt and pepper

warm crusty bread, to serve
   (optional)

- Place the tomatoes in a heatproof bowl and pour over boiling water to cover. Leave for 1–2 minutes, then drain, cut a cross at the stem end of each tomato and peel off the skins. Cut into quarters, remove the seeds and cut the flesh into thick strips. Place in a large, shallow bowl and add the preserved lemon rind.

- Add the onion, capers and herbs to the bowl. Gently toss with the oil and lemon juice and season. Sprinkle over the paprika and serve with warm crusty bread, if liked.

 Spicy Tomato and Preserved Lemon Salad Thinly slice 4–6 ripe tomatoes and place in a shallow bowl. Add 2 deseeded and finely sliced large green chillies and the finely sliced rind of ½ preserved lemon (see page 68). Drizzle over a little olive or argan oil and season with salt. Gently stir in a finely chopped small bunch of coriander and serve.

 Spicy Roasted Tomatoes with Preserved Lemon Tip 450 g (14½ oz) cherry tomatoes into an ovenproof dish and pour over 2–3 tablespoons olive oil. Place in a preheated oven, 180°C (350°F), Gas Mark 4, for 15 minutes. Add 1–2 finely chopped red chillies or 1–2 teaspoons chopped dried red chilli and 1 teaspoon sugar and mix together with the tomatoes and oil. Return to the oven and cook for a further 10 minutes until the tomatoes begin to buckle. Season with salt and spoon onto a serving dish. Scatter over the finely chopped rind of ½ preserved lemon (see page 68) and garnish with a finely chopped small bunch of coriander.

 # Sweet Cucumber and Orange Blossom Salad

Serves 4

2 cucumbers, peeled and grated
juice of ½ lemon
1–2 tablespoons orange
  blossom water
1–2 teaspoons sugar or
  runny honey
salt
½ teaspoon ground cinnamon,
  for dusting

- Place the grated cucumber in a colander, sprinkle with salt and leave to stand for about 5 minutes. Using your hands, squeeze out the excess water and place the cucumber in a bowl.

- Mix together the lemon juice, orange blossom water and sugar or honey in a separate bowl, then pour over the cucumber. Toss well, cover and chill for 10 minutes. Just before serving, dust with the cinnamon.

 ### Salted Cucumber Fingers

Peel the skin off 2 cucumbers in strips, leaving some narrow strips on the flesh for decorative effect. Cut into equal-sized thick fingers. Place on a plate, sprinkle with 1–2 teaspoons coarse salt and leave to stand for 5–6 minutes until the salt has almost dissolved. Lift the cucumber off the plate leaving behind any excess liquid, but don't rinse. Arrange in a fan on a serving dish and serve immediately.

Cucumber, Pomegranate and Orange Blossom Salad

Peel 1 cucumber, cut it into quarters lengthways and finely slice. Tip into a colander, sprinkle with salt and leave to stand for 10 minutes. Meanwhile, cut 1 white onion into bite-sized pieces, tip into a separate colander, sprinkle with salt and leave to stand for 5 minutes. Cut 2 pomegranates into quarters then, holding them over a plate to catch the juice, bend each quarter backwards and flick the seeds into a serving bowl, leaving behind the white membrane and pith (this takes about 10 minutes). Add any pomegranate juice to the bowl. Rinse and drain the cucumber, then squeeze out the excess water. Rinse and drain the onion, then pat dry with kitchen paper. Add the cucumber and onion to the pomegranate seeds and juice, then toss with 2 tablespoons orange blossom water. Leave to stand for 5–10 minutes to let the juices mingle with the syrup. Just before serving, toss in 1 tablespoon finely shredded mint.

30 Orange, Date and Chilli Salad

Serves 4

3–4 ripe sweet oranges

150 g (5 oz) ready-to-eat soft pitted dates, finely sliced

2–3 tablespoons orange blossom water

1 red chilli, deseeded and finely sliced

finely sliced rind of ½ preserved lemon (see page 68)

- Using a sharp knife, remove the peel and pith from the oranges. Place the oranges on a plate to catch the juice and thinly slice into circles or half moons, removing any seeds. Place the oranges and juice in a shallow bowl.

- Scatter over the dates, then pour over the orange blossom water. Cover and leave to stand for 15 minutes to let the flavours mingle and the dates soften.

- Scatter over the chilli and preserved lemon rind and gently toss together.

 Orange, Olive and Chilli Salad

Using a sharp knife, remove the peel and pith from 3 oranges, then thinly slice into circles or half moons, removing any seeds, and arrange on a serving plate. Finely slice 1 red onion into circles or half moons and arrange over the oranges. Drizzle over a little olive oil and season with salt. Scatter over 2 tablespoons black olives and garnish with 1 deseeded and finely sliced green chilli and a finely shredded small bunch of mint.

 Orange, Radish and Chilli Salad

Using a sharp knife, remove the peel and pith from 2–3 oranges. Holding the oranges over a bowl to catch the juice, cut down between the membranes and remove the segments. Cut each segment in half, remove any seeds and place in the bowl. Dry-fry 2 teaspoons fennel seeds in a small, heavy-based frying pan over a medium heat for 2–3 minutes until they emit a nutty aroma, then scatter over the oranges. Add 6–8 sliced small red radishes, 1 tablespoon pitted and sliced green olives and 2 deseeded and sliced green chillies. Mix together 2 tablespoons olive oil, 1 tablespoon orange blossom water and 1 teaspoon runny honey and pour over the salad. Season, toss together lightly and serve scattered with 1 tablespoon finely chopped parsley.

MOR-STAR-MUY

Artichoke, Clementine and Preserved Lemon Salad

Serves 4

4 canned artichoke hearts, rinsed and drained

3–4 sweet clementines, peeled and pith removed

1–2 tablespoons orange blossom water

finely sliced rind of ½ preserved lemon (see page 68)

- Cut the artichoke hearts in half lengthways, then pull them apart into delicate leaves. Place the clementines on a plate to catch the juice and thinly slice into circles, removing any seeds. Cut into quarters.

- Arrange the artichokes and clementines in a shallow serving bowl. Splash over the orange blossom water and any clementine juice and add the preserved lemon rind. Toss together just before serving.

---

 2 Artichoke, Egg and Preserved Lemon Salad Place 4 ready-prepared fresh or frozen artichoke bottoms and the juice of ½ lemon in a saucepan of boiling water and cook for 10 minutes. Meanwhile, boil 2 eggs in a separate saucepan of boiling water for 6–7 minutes, then drain and refresh under cold running water. Drain and refresh the artichokes, then place upside down to drain. Shell the eggs and cut into quarters. Cut the artichokes into thick slices, then arrange both on a serving dish. Scatter over 2–3 teaspoons rinsed and drained baby capers and the finely sliced rind of ½ preserved lemon (see page 68). Mix together 2 tablespoons olive oil, 1 tablespoon cider vinegar, 1 teaspoon runny honey, 1 crushed garlic clove and salt and pepper, then pour over the salad.

3 Ginger, Honey and Preserved Lemon Artichokes Fill a bowl with cold water and stir in the juice of 1 lemon. Remove the leaves from 4 fresh globe artichokes, cut off the stems, scoop out the choke and all the hairy bits, then trim the bottoms. Place in the water to prevent them turning brown. Bring a large saucepan of water and ½ teaspoon salt to the boil, then drop in the artichoke bottoms and cook for 10 minutes until just tender to the point of a knife. Meanwhile, put a pinch of saffron threads into a small bowl, cover with 2 tablespoons water and set aside. Drain the artichokes, refresh under cold running water and drain again, then cut into quarters. Heat 2–3 tablespoons olive oil in a heavy-based saucepan, stir in 2 crushed garlic cloves and 25 g (1 oz) fresh root ginger, peeled and finely chopped, and cook for 1–2 minutes. Add the saffron water and 1–2 tablespoons honey and stir for 1 minute, then toss in the artichokes, coating them well. Pour in about 100 ml (3½ fl oz) water, season and sprinkle over the finely sliced rind of 1 preserved lemon (see page 68). Cover and cook gently for 5–10 minutes, turning the artichokes once or twice, until very tender. Garnish with a finely chopped small bunch of flat leaf parsley and serve warm or at room temperature.

 # Beetroot, Apple and Orange Blossom Salad

Serves 4

2 beetroot, peeled and grated

1 crisp green apple, cored and grated

juice of ½ lemon

2 tablespoons orange blossom water

salt

- Mix together the beetroot and apple in a serving bowl.

- Add the lemon juice and orange blossom water and season with salt. Toss together well and serve.

 Beetroot, Orange, Egg and Anchovy Salad Cook 3 eggs in a saucepan of boiling water for 6 minutes. Meanwhile, put 12–16 shop-bought ready-cooked baby beetroot into a shallow bowl. Add 1 orange, peeled, cut into quarters and thinly sliced. Drain the eggs and refresh under cold running water, then shell and cut into quarters. Arrange around the beetroot and orange. Top with 12 preserved anchovy fillets, rinsed and drained. Dry-fry 2 teaspoons coriander seeds in a small, heavy-based frying pan over a medium heat for 2 minutes until they emit a nutty aroma. Using a pestle and mortar, crush the seeds. Mix together 2 tablespoons olive oil, the juice of 1 lemon, the crushed coriander seeds, 1 teaspoon thyme leaves and 1 teaspoon runny honey. Season and pour over the salad.

Roasted Beetroot, Orange and Cinnamon Salad Place 500 g (1 lb) shop-bought ready-cooked beetroot, cut into quarters, 4–6 cardamom pods and 1–2 teaspoons fennel seeds in an ovenproof dish. Toss with 2 tablespoons olive oil and roast in a preheated oven, 200°C (400°F), Gas Mark 6, for 15 minutes. Meanwhile, using a sharp knife, remove the peel and pith from 2 oranges. Holding the oranges over a bowl to catch the juice, cut down between the membranes and remove the segments. Place in the bowl and set aside. Drizzle 1–2 teaspoons runny honey over the beetroot, then return to the oven and cook for a further 5–10 minutes. Tip the beetroot and all the sweet roasting juices into a bowl. Pop the seeds out of the cardamom pods and add the seeds to the beetroot, discarding the pods.

Toss with 2 tablespoons orange blossom water, season and add the orange segments and juice. Dust with 1 teaspoon ground cinnamon and serve.

3️⃣0️⃣ Warm Garlicky Lentil Salad

Serves 4

3 tablespoons olive or argan oil
1 red onion, finely chopped
1 teaspoon sugar
2 teaspoons turmeric
1 teaspoon ground cumin
1 teaspoon ground coriander
175 g (6 oz) brown or green
   lentils, rinsed, picked over
   and drained
about 850 ml (1½ pints) water
3–4 garlic cloves, finely sliced
1 tablespoon brown mustard seeds
juice of 1 lemon
small bunch of coriander,
   finely chopped
salt and pepper
lemon wedges, to serve

- Heat 2 tablespoons of the oil in a large, heavy-based saucepan, stir in the onion and sugar and cook for 2–3 minutes until just beginning to colour. Stir in the ground spices, then add the lentils. Pour in the measurement water and stir well.

- Bring to the boil, reduce the heat and simmer for 20 minutes, or until the lentils are tender and all the liquid has been absorbed. Tip the lentils into a shallow serving bowl.

- Heat the remaining oil in a frying pan, stir in the garlic and mustard seeds and cook for 2–3 minutes until they begin to colour.

- Add to the lentils with the lemon juice and most of the chopped coriander. Season well and toss until well mixed. Scatter over the remaining coriander and serve warm with lemon wedges to squeeze over.

 Lentils with Spicy Garlic Dressing
Place a 250 g (8 oz) pouch of ready-cooked lentils in a serving bowl. Add 1 large red onion, sliced into bite-sized pieces, and a finely chopped small bunch of coriander. Mix together 2–3 tablespoons olive or argan oil, the juice of 1 lemon, 1–2 deseeded and finely chopped red or green chillies, 25 g (1 oz) fresh root ginger, peeled and finely chopped, 2–3 crushed garlic cloves and 1 teaspoon runny honey. Season well with salt and pour over the lentils. Toss well and serve.

 Garlicky Lentil, Carrot and Sultana Salad Rinse, pick over and drain 150 g (5 oz) brown, green or Puy lentils, then cook in a saucepan of boiling water for 10–15 minutes, or until they are tender but not mushy. Meanwhile, soak 2 tablespoons sultanas in 2 tablespoons orange blossom water. Drain the lentils, refresh under cold running water and drain again, then tip into a serving bowl. Add 4 peeled and grated carrots, the soaked sultanas, 1–2 teaspoons caraway seeds and a roughly chopped small bunch of flat leaf parsley.

Mix together 2–3 tablespoons olive oil, 2 tablespoons balsamic vinegar, 2 crushed garlic cloves and 1 teaspoon runny honey in a bowl and season. Pour over the salad and toss well.

10 Spicy Paprika Chickpeas

Serves 4

1 tablespoon ghee
1 teaspoon cumin seeds
1 teaspoon coriander seeds
2 garlic cloves, chopped
225 g (7½ oz) canned chickpeas,
   rinsed and drained
1 teaspoon turmeric
1 teaspoon chilli powder
1–2 teaspoons dried thyme
1 teaspoon smoked paprika
salt
flatbread, to serve

- Heat the ghee in a heavy-based frying pan, stir in the cumin seeds, coriander seeds and garlic and cook for 2–3 minutes until the garlic begins to colour.

- Toss in the chickpeas and cook for 1–2 minutes, stirring to coat in the spices. Stir in the turmeric and chilli powder and cook for a further 1–2 minutes, stirring continuously to prevent the spices burning.

- Sprinkle with the thyme and paprika and season with salt. Tip into a serving bowl and serve warm with flatbread.

20 Chickpea, Sesame and Paprika Dip

Using a large pestle and mortar, pound a 400 g (13 oz) can chickpeas, rinsed and drained, 2 garlic cloves and 1 teaspoon cumin seeds to a coarse paste. Dry-fry 1 tablespoon sesame seeds in a small, heavy-based frying pan over a medium heat for 2–3 minutes until golden brown. Stir most of the seeds into the paste, then mix with 3–4 tablespoons olive oil and the juice of 1 lemon. Season well and spoon into a bowl. Drizzle over a little olive oil, scatter over the remaining toasted sesame seeds and dust with paprika. Serve with strips of toasted pitta bread.

30 Chickpea Salad with Onion, Eggs and

Paprika Heat 2–3 tablespoons olive oil in a heavy-based frying pan and stir in 1–2 teaspoons cumin seeds and 1 onion, sliced, for 4–5 minutes, until the onions begin to colour. Toss in a 400 g (13 oz) can chickpeas, rinsed and drained, and cook for 2–3 minutes, then tip them into a bowl. Add 2–3 crushed garlic cloves, the juice of 1 lemon and 1–2 teaspoons paprika. Season the chickpeas to taste with sea salt and black pepper and toss in a small bunch of flat leaf parsley, coarsely chopped, and a small bunch of mint, coarsely chopped, reserving a little for garnishing. Leave the chickpeas to cool for 10–15 minutes and season to taste. Heat a further 1 tablespoon olive oil in a heavy-based pan and crack in 4 eggs. Cook them for 3–4 minutes, until the white is firm, and lift them onto the chickpeas. Sprinkle a little paprika over them and garnish with the reserved herbs.

30 Spicy Sweet Potato and Coriander Salad

Serves 4

2–3 tablespoons olive or argan oil

1 red onion, roughly chopped

1 teaspoon cumin seeds

25 g (1 oz) fresh root ginger, peeled and grated

2 orange-fleshed sweet potatoes, peeled and cubed

2–3 tablespoons orange blossom water

finely sliced or chopped rind of 1 preserved lemon (see page 68)

small bunch of coriander, finely chopped

8 green olives stuffed with red pimento, left whole or halved

salt and pepper

- Heat the oil in a large, heavy-based frying pan, stir in the onion, cumin seeds and ginger and cook for 2–3 minutes. Toss in the sweet potatoes and cook for 1–2 minutes, then pour in just enough water to cover the base of the pan.

- Cover and cook gently for about 10 minutes until the sweet potatoes are tender but firm and the liquid has been absorbed. Tip into a shallow bowl, pour over the orange blossom water and leave to cool.

- Add most of the preserved lemon rind and coriander to the sweet potatoes, season and gently toss together. Add the green olives and sprinkle over the remaining preserved lemon and coriander. Serve at room temperature.

 Sweet Potato and Coriander Relish

Peel and grate 2 sweet potatoes and place in a bowl. Pour over the juice of 1 lemon and stir in the grated rind of 1 small orange and 1 tablespoon very finely chopped coriander. Season well with salt and serve with spicy dishes and syrupy tagines.

 Sautéed Coriander Sweet Potatoes

Peel and cube 2 sweet potatoes. Steam for 10 minutes until just tender. Heat 1–2 tablespoons olive or argan oil or 1 tablespoon ghee in a heavy-based frying pan, stir in 2 finely chopped garlic cloves, 1 deseeded and finely chopped green or red chilli, 1 tablespoon peeled and finely chopped fresh root ginger, 2 teaspoons coriander seeds and 1 teaspoon sugar and cook for 2–3 minutes. Add the steamed sweet potato and cook, stirring, for a further 2–3 minutes. Season and scatter over a finely chopped small bunch of coriander. Mix together 4–6 tablespoons natural yogurt, 1 crushed garlic clove and salt and pepper in a bowl and serve with the sweet potatoes.

30 Roasted Courgette, Apple and Clementine Salad

Serves 4–6

2 courgettes, halved and thinly
  sliced lengthways
1 crisp green or red apple, cored
  and thinly sliced
2–3 tablespoons olive oil
1 tablespoon runny honey
2 teaspoons fennel seeds
2 sweet clementines, peeled and
  pith removed
juice of 1 lemon
finely sliced rind of ½ preserved
  lemon (see page 68)
salt

- Place the courgettes and apple in a baking dish and spoon over the oil. Place in a preheated oven, 200°C (400°F), Gas Mark 6, for about 15 minutes. Drizzle over the honey, then return to the oven and cook for a further 5–10 minutes until softened and slightly golden.

- Meanwhile, dry-fry the fennel seeds in a small, heavy-based frying pan over a medium heat for 2–3 minutes until they emit a nutty aroma. Set aside.

- Place the clementines on a plate to catch the juice and thinly slice into circles, removing any seeds. Arrange the slices in a serving dish and spoon the roasted courgette and apple on top.

- Stir any clementine juice into the roasting juices in the baking dish. Add the lemon juice and season with a little salt. Drizzle over the salad and scatter with the toasted fennel seeds and preserved lemon rind. Serve warm or at room temperature.

 Baby Courgettes and Apple with Dukkah Dip Mix together 2 tablespoons ready-made dukkah spice mix, 2 crushed garlic cloves, 1 finely chopped red chilli, 2 tablespoons olive oil, the juice of 1 lemon and a finely chopped small bunch of coriander in a small bowl. Season with salt and serve with 4 halved baby courgettes and 1 cored apple, cut into segments, for dipping.

 Courgette, Apple and Lime Salad Place 2 thinly sliced courgettes and 1 cored and thinly sliced green apple in a bowl. Pour over the juice of 1 lime. Remove the rind from another lime and, using a sharp knife, cut down between the membranes and remove the segments, then add them to the bowl. Sprinkle over 1 scant teaspoon sugar, season with salt and add 1–2 tablespoons finely shredded mint leaves. Toss well, garnish with a little more shredded mint and serve.

MOR-STAR-PEC

30 Grilled Peppers with Feta

Serves 4

3 red, green or yellow peppers
200 g (7 oz) goats' or feta
  cheese, crumbled
1 red onion, finely chopped
small bunch of parsley,
  finely chopped
finely chopped or shredded
  rind of 1 preserved lemon
  (see page 68)
1–2 tablespoons argan or olive oil
flatbread, to serve

- Place the peppers directly over a gas flame or under a preheated hot grill for 10–15 minutes, turning occasionally, until buckled and charred. Place in a plastic food bag to sweat for 2–3 minutes, then hold by the stalks under cold running water and carefully peel off the skins. Place on a board, remove the stalks and seeds, then finely slice the flesh.

- Tip the peppers into a shallow bowl and scatter over the crumbled cheese.

- In a separate bowl, mix together the onion, parsley and preserved lemon rind, then scatter over the peppers. Drizzle over the oil and serve with flatbread.

---

10 Pickled Green Peppers

Wash 8 long green Mediterranean peppers and pat dry, then tightly pack into a large sterilized jar. Mix together 300 ml (½ pint) water, 300 ml (½ pint) white wine vinegar and 1 scant tablespoon salt, then pour over the peppers, making sure they are submerged – add more vinegar if necessary. Tightly seal with a vinegar-proof lid and store in the refrigerator for at least 2 weeks before using. (The peppers can also be stored in the refrigerator for 4–6 weeks.)

20 Red Pepper Paste

Deseed and chop 2 long red Mediterranean peppers and 2 red chillies, place in a food processor with 1–2 tablespoons olive oil, 1 tablespoon granulated sugar, 1 teaspoon fennel seeds, 1 teaspoon sea salt and a splash of balsamic vinegar and whizz together. Tip the mixture into a heavy-based frying pan and heat until bubbling, stirring continuously. Reduce the heat and simmer for about 15 minutes until thick. Serve as a warm dip or use as a condiment or sauce. (The cooled paste can also be stored in a sealed sterilized jar in the refrigerator for 1–2 weeks.)

 # Pear, Chicory and Rose Petal Salad

Serves 4

2 ripe but firm pears, peeled, cored and thinly sliced

juice of ½ lemon

1–2 tablespoons rosewater

2 heads of white or red chicory, leaves separated and rinsed

1 tablespoon olive oil

1 teaspoon runny honey

small handful of fresh, scented rose petals

salt

- Place the pears in a bowl and lightly toss with the lemon juice and rosewater. Leave to stand for 5 minutes.

- Arrange the chicory leaves in a shallow salad bowl. Remove the pear from the rosewater and lemon juice with a slotted spoon and scatter it over and around the chicory leaves.

- Mix the oil with any rosewater and lemon juice left in the bowl and pour over the salad. Drizzle over the honey and sprinkle with salt. Scatter over the rose petals and toss just before serving.

 ### Chicory, Peach and Rosewater Salad

Trim 2 heads of red or white chicory, separate the leaves, then rinse and drain. Peel, halve and stone 2 ripe but firm peaches. Slice each half into 4 segments. Arrange the chicory leaves and peach slices in a shallow dish. Scatter over the finely sliced rind of ½ preserved lemon (see page 68) and pour over 2 tablespoons rosewater. Toss gently just before serving.

 ### Pickled Pears with Rose Petals

Place 100 ml (3½ fl oz) water, 300 ml (½ pint) white wine or cider vinegar, 2 tablespoons honey, 2 cinnamon sticks, 6–8 allspice berries and a pinch of saffron threads in a heavy-based saucepan and bring to the boil, stirring continuously until the honey has dissolved. Peel 4 pears, keeping the stalks intact, halve lengthways and add to the pan. Bring back to the boil, then reduce the heat and poach gently for 15–20 minutes until tender but still firm. Remove the pears and place in a sterilized jar. Pour over the hot liquid and leave to cool. Seal with a vinegar-proof lid and store in a cool place or the refrigerator for 2–3 weeks before using. Serve garnished with fresh rose petals. (The pickled pears can also be stored in the refrigerator for 4–6 weeks.)

MOR-STAR-JOW

30 Apricot and Apple Chutney with Pan-Fried Haloumi

Serves 4

225 g (7½ oz) ready-to-eat
   dried apricots, chopped
1 tart green apple, peeled,
   cored and chopped
1 onion, finely chopped
2–3 garlic cloves, finely chopped
1 tablespoon peeled and grated
   fresh root ginger
1 tablespoon sultanas
2 cinnamon sticks
grated rind and juice of 1 lemon
150 ml (¼ pint) white wine vinegar
pinch of chilli powder
120 g (4 oz) granulated sugar
1 tablespoon honey
2–3 tablespoons orange
   blossom water
2–3 tablespoons sunflower oil
225 g (7½ oz) haloumi cheese,
   thickly sliced
salt

- To make the chutney, put the apricots, apple, onion, garlic, ginger, sultanas, cinnamon, lemon rind and juice, vinegar, chilli powder and sugar into a heavy-based saucepan and bring to the boil, stirring continuously, then cook over a medium heat for 20 minutes, stirring occasionally, until thick.

- Add the honey and orange blossom water and cook gently for a further 5–10 minutes until thick and fragrant, then season with salt.

- Meanwhile, heat the oil in a heavy-based frying pan, add the haloumi and fry for 3–4 minutes, turning once, until golden brown. Drain on kitchen paper. Serve immediately with the chutney.

 Apricot and Apple Yogurt Dip

Peel, core and thinly slice or grate 1 crisp apple and toss with the juice of ½ lemon. In a separate bowl, beat together 6–8 tablespoons thick natural yogurt and 2 crushed garlic cloves and season. Fold 150 g (5 oz) ready-to-eat dried apricots, cut into thin strips, and the apple into the yogurt and serve with chunks of warm crusty bread.

 Apricot, Apple and Almond Salad

Place 175 g (6 oz) whole almonds in a bowl, pour over boiling water to just cover, then leave to soak for 5–10 minutes. Meanwhile, put 175 g (6 oz) ready-to-eat dried apricots, cut into thin strips, and 1 cored crisp apple, sliced into thin strips, into a separate bowl. Pour in the juice of 1 lemon and 2 tablespoons orange blossom water and toss well. Drain and rinse the almonds, then rub off the skins with your fingers. Slice the almonds into thin sticks and toss with the apricots and apple.

30 Warm Stuffed Dates with Spiced Syrup

Serves 4

12 ready-to-eat soft pitted dates

12 walnut halves

1–2 tablespoons ghee or butter

2 tablespoons pomegranate syrup

2 tablespoons granulated sugar

1 cinnamon stick

seeds of 4 cardamom pods

2–3 cloves

2–3 tablespoons orange
blossom water

salt

small bunch of flat leaf parsley,
finely chopped, to garnish

- Find the opening in each pitted date and stuff it with a walnut half.

- Melt the ghee or butter in a heavy-based frying pan, add the stuffed dates and cook for 2–3 minutes, turning occasionally. Stir in the pomegranate syrup, sugar, spices and enough water to just cover the base of the pan. Splash in the orange blossom water and heat until bubbling. Reduce the heat, cover and simmer for about 15 minutes.

- Remove the lid and simmer for a further 5 minutes, adding a little more orange blossom water if necessary. Season with salt and transfer the stuffed dates to a serving dish. Drizzle over the syrupy juice, garnish with the parsley and serve hot or at room temperature.

---

1 Pickled Fresh Dates

Pack 225 g (7½ oz) pitted fresh dates into a sterilized jar. Place 300 ml (½ pint) cider vinegar, 2 tablespoons muscovado sugar, 2 cinnamon sticks, 2 dried red chillies and the seeds of 4–6 cardamom pods in a heavy-based saucepan and bring to the boil, stirring continuously. Reduce the heat and simmer for about 8 minutes. Pour over the dates, seal with a vinegar-proof lid and leave to cool. Store in the refrigerator for 1–2 weeks before using. (The pickled dates can also be stored in the refrigerator for 3–4 weeks.)

2 Date Relish

Heat 1 tablespoon olive oil in a frying pan, stir in 1 finely chopped red onion, 2 finely chopped garlic cloves and 1 teaspoon cumin seeds and cook for 2–3 minutes until the onion begins to colour. Toss in 3 tablespoons finely chopped ready-to-eat pitted dates, 2 teaspoons finely chopped Pickled Red Chillies (see page 70) and 1–2 teaspoons muscovado sugar and cook for another 2–3 minutes. Stir in 4 tablespoons pomegranate syrup and cook the mixture gently for a further 2–3 minutes. Season with salt, toss in 2 tablespoons fresh pomegranate seeds and leave to cool. Serve with toasted flatbreads or cheese.

30 Mixed Pickled Vegetables

Serves 4

1 small cucumber
1 teaspoon salt
2 carrots, peeled
1 large white radish, peeled
1 red pepper, cored and deseeded
2 tablespoons blanched almonds
2 teaspoons pink peppercorns
1–2 teaspoons cumin seeds
pinch of saffron threads
1–2 cinnamon sticks
juice of 2 lemons
1–2 tablespoons cider vinegar
1 tablespoon granulated sugar
1–2 tablespoons orange
   blossom water
2 tablespoons finely chopped
   coriander

- Peel and deseed the cucumber, then cut into matchsticks and place in a colander, sprinkle with the salt and leave to stand for 5 minutes. Rinse, drain and pat dry, then place in a large, non-metallic bowl.

- Cut the carrots, radish and red pepper into matchsticks. Add to the cucumber with the almonds and spices, then stir in the lemon juice, vinegar, sugar and orange blossom water. Cover and chill for 15–20 minutes. Just before serving, toss in the coriander.

- (The pickles can also be stored in a sterilized jar, sealed with a vinegar-proof lid, in the refrigerator for 3–4 weeks.)

1 Pickled Purple Turnips

Trim and peel 8 small white turnips, then rinse and pat dry. Pack into a sterilized jar with 4 peeled garlic cloves and 2 slices of raw beetroot. Mix together 300 ml (½ pint) white wine vinegar, 300 ml (½ pint) water and 1 teaspoon sea salt, then pour over the turnips. Seal with a vinegar-proof lid and store for 1–2 weeks until the turnips have taken on a purplish-pink hue. (The pickled turnips can also be stored in the refrigerator for 3–4 weeks.)

2 Pickled Stuffed Cabbage Leaves

Place 8 white or green cabbage leaves in a steamer and cook for 5–6 minutes until softened. Refresh under cold running water and drain well. Place the leaves on a flat surface and remove the central ribs so that the leaves lie flat. Using a pestle and mortar, pound 3 garlic cloves and 3 tablespoons walnuts to a coarse paste. Stir in 1 finely chopped red chilli and 2 teaspoons finely chopped preserved lemon rind (see page 68). Mix with 1 tablespoon olive oil, then place a teaspoonful of the mixture near the top of each leaf. Pull the top edge over the mixture, tuck in the sides and roll the leaf into a tight log. Tightly pack the stuffed leaves into a non-metallic bowl or sterilized jar and pour over 300 ml (½ pint) white wine or cider vinegar combined with a little salt. Cover the bowl or jar and store in the refrigerator for 1–2 weeks before use. (The pickled stuffed cabbage leaves can also be stored in the refrigerator for 3–4 weeks.)

20 Preserved Lemons

Serves 4

8–10 organic unwaxed lemons, washed and dried

about 10 tablespoons sea salt

juice of 3–4 lemons

- Slice the ends off each lemon and stand them on one end. Using a small, sharp knife, carefully make 2 vertical cuts three-quarters of the way through each lemon, as if cutting into quarters, but keep the bases intact. Stuff 1 tablespoon of the salt into each lemon, then pack into a large sterilized jar and seal tightly. Store in a cool place for 3–4 days to soften the skins.

- Press the lemons down into the jar until tightly packed, then cover with the lemon juice. Seal the jar and store in a cool place for at least 1 month before use. Keep for 3–4 months.

- To use, rinse off the salt and pat dry with kitchen paper. Cut the lemon into quarters and, using a small, sharp knife, remove the flesh, seeds and pith. Finely slice or chop the rind and use as required.

---

10 Pickled Lemons

Pack 8–10 small unwaxed lemons into a sterilized jar. Place 600 ml (1 pint) white wine vinegar, 2–3 tablespoons granulated sugar, 1 tablespoon coriander seeds, 2 dried sage sprigs and 2–3 dried red chillies in a small, heavy-based saucepan and bring to the boil, stirring continuously until the sugar has dissolved, then reduce the heat and simmer for 5 minutes. Pour over the lemons, seal with a vinegar-proof lid and leave to cool. Store in the refrigerator for 2 weeks before using. (The pickled lemons can also be stored in the refrigerator for 4–6 weeks.)

30 Lemon and Herb Jam

Peel and finely shred the rind of 4 unwaxed lemons, then halve the flesh and squeeze the juice. Put the rind into a small, heavy-based saucepan with 1 tablespoon peeled and finely chopped fresh root ginger, 1 teaspoon coriander seeds and 1 teaspoon finely chopped dried red chilli. Add the lemon juice, 75 ml (3 fl oz) cider vinegar and 2 tablespoons granulated sugar, then heat until bubbling, stirring continuously until the sugar has dissolved. Reduce the heat and simmer for 15–20 minutes until the mixture is almost dry, making sure the sugar doesn't burn. Season with a little salt and leave to cool in the pan. Toss in 1 tablespoon each of finely chopped coriander and mint and serve with bread and cheese.

MOR-STAR-SAF

Roasted Chilli Harissa Paste

Serves 4 (a little goes a long way)

12 large fresh red chillies, such as Guajillo, Mexican Horn or New Mexico

3 tablespoons olive oil

1 teaspoon cumin seed

1 teaspoon coriander seeds

1 teaspoon caraway or fennel seeds

3–4 garlic cloves, chopped

1 teaspoon sea salt

1 tablespoon finely chopped coriander

crudités or toasted flatbreads, to serve

- Place the chillies in an ovenproof dish, pour over the oil and roast in a preheated oven, 200°C (400°F), Gas Mark 6, for 20–25 minutes until the skins begin to buckle. Meanwhile, dry-fry all the seeds in a small, heavy-based frying pan over a medium heat for 2–3 minutes until they emit a nutty aroma, then grind in a spice grinder.

- Using a small, sharp knife, remove the stalks and skins from the roasted chillies. Slit lengthways and scrape out the seeds. Using a pestle and mortar, pound the chilli flesh, garlic and salt to a smooth paste. Add the spices, mix with 2–3 tablespoons of the roasting oil and stir in the coriander.

- Spoon the harissa into a small bowl, drizzle over a little more roasting oil and serve with crudités or toasted flatbread. Alternatively, put into a sterilized jar, top with a thin layer of olive oil and seal. (The harissa paste can also be stored in the refrigerator for up to 4 weeks.)

 Pickled Red Chillies

Using a small, sharp knife, slit 8 red Guajillo or Serrano chillies lengthways, without cutting right through, and pack into a sterilized jar. Place 400 ml (14 fl oz) white wine vinegar, 2 tablespoons granulated sugar and 2 teaspoons each of sea salt and coriander seeds in a saucepan and bring to the boil, stirring until the sugar has dissolved. Pour over the chillies to cover, seal with a vinegar-proof lid and leave to cool. Store in the refrigerator for at least 2 weeks before using. (The chillies can also be stored in the refrigerator for 4–6 weeks.)

Dried Chilli Dukkah Dip

Dry-fry 1 tablespoon dried chilli flakes in a heavy-based frying pan over a medium heat for 2 minutes, then remove and set aside. Using the same pan, dry-fry 2 tablespoons each of hazelnuts and sunflower seeds, 1 tablespoon sesame seeds and 2 teaspoons each of cumin seeds and coriander seeds for 2–3 minutes until they emit a nutty aroma. Using a pestle and mortar, pound the nuts and seeds with 1 teaspoon sea salt to a paste. Heat 2 tablespoons olive oil in the pan, stir in 2 crushed garlic cloves and the chilli flakes and cook for 2 minutes until the garlic begins to colour. Stir the oil into the nut mixture and mix well, then stir in the juice of ½ lemon. Spoon into a bowl and leave to stand for 10 minutes to let the flavours mingle. Serve with toasted flatbreads or crudités.

QuickCook

Soups, Pastries and Savoury Snacks

Recipes listed by cooking time

30

20

10

30 Tomato, Ras el Hanout and Vermicelli Soup

Serves 4

8 large ripe tomatoes
2–3 tablespoons olive or argan oil
4 cloves
2 onions, chopped
2 celery sticks, chopped
1 carrot, peeled and chopped
1–2 teaspoons sugar
1 tablespoon tomato purée
1–2 teaspoons ras el hanout
large bunch of coriander,
 finely chopped
1.5 litres (2½ pints) hot vegetable
 stock
120 g (4 oz) fine vermicelli,
 broken into small pieces
salt and pepper
chunks of crusty bread, to serve
 (optional)

- Place the tomatoes in a heatproof bowl and pour over boiling water to cover. Leave for 1–2 minutes, then drain, cut a cross at the stem end of each tomato and peel off the skins. Roughly chop and set aside.

- Meanwhile, heat the oil in a heavy-based saucepan, stir in the cloves, onions, celery and carrot and cook for 3–4 minutes until they begin to colour. Add the tomatoes and sugar and cook over a medium heat for 4–5 minutes until the mixture is thick.

- Stir in the tomato purée, ras el hanout and most of the coriander. Pour in the stock and bring to the boil, then cook over a medium heat for 15 minutes. Stir in the vermicelli, season and cook for a further 5–6 minutes until the pasta is just tender.

- Garnish with the remaining coriander and ladle into serving bowls. Serve with crusty bread, if liked.

 Quick Tomato and Ras el Hanout Pasta
Heat 1 tablespoon olive oil and a knob of butter in a heavy-based saucepan, stir in 1 crushed garlic clove and 1 teaspoon crushed coriander seeds and cook for 1–2 minutes. Stir in 1–2 teaspoons ras el hanout and 1 teaspoon sugar, add 400 g (13 oz) passata and cook over a low heat for 6–8 minutes. Season with salt and black pepper and swirl in 1 tablespoon olive oil with a finely chopped small bunch of coriander. Serve the sauce spooned over cooked fresh pasta.

 Puréed Tomato and Ras el Hanout Soup Heat 2 tablespoons olive oil and a knob of butter in a heavy-based saucepan, add 2 chopped onions and 1 teaspoon sugar and cook, stirring, for 2–3 minutes until the onions are soft and begin to colour. Stir in 2 teaspoons tomato purée and 2 teaspoons ras el hanout, add a 400 g (13 oz) can chopped tomatoes and 900 ml (32 fl oz) hot vegetable stock and bring to the boil, then cook over a medium heat for 10 minutes. Purée the soup with a hand-held blender or whizz in a blender. Return to the heat and season to taste. Garnish with a little finely chopped coriander and serve with crusty bread.

MOR-SOUP-FED

30 Honeyed Pumpkin and Ginger Broth

Serves 4

2 tablespoons olive oil

15 g (½ oz) butter

1 onion, finely chopped

50 g (2 oz) fresh root ginger, peeled and finely chopped

2 dried red chillies

2–3 celery sticks, cut into bite-sized pieces

700 g (1½ lb) peeled and deseeded pumpkin, cut into bite-sized chunks

1 litre (1¾ pints) hot chicken or vegetable stock

small bunch of flat leaf parsley, finely chopped

1–2 tablespoons honey

salt and pepper

- Heat the oil and butter in a large, heavy-based saucepan, stir in the onion and ginger and cook for 2–3 minutes until they begin to colour. Add the chillies, celery and pumpkin and cook for 1–2 minutes, stirring to coat well.

- Pour in the stock and bring to the boil, then reduce the heat and cook gently for 20–25 minutes until the vegetables are tender. Season and stir in most of the parsley.

- Meanwhile, in a small saucepan, gently heat the honey until it begins to bubble. Ladle the broth into serving bowls, drizzle over the hot honey and garnish with the remaining parsley.

 Pumpkin and Ginger Butter Dip

Melt 50 g (2 oz) butter in a heavy-based saucepan, stir in 25 g (1 oz) peeled and grated fresh root ginger and cook over a low heat for 1–2 minutes. Stir in 640 g (1 lb 7 oz) canned pumpkin purée and cook for 2 minutes until heated through, then season. Serve with chunks of crusty bread.

 Puréed Pumpkin and Ginger Soup

Heat 2 tablespoons olive oil and a knob of butter in a heavy-based saucepan, stir in 1 chopped onion, 25 g (1 oz) peeled and chopped fresh root ginger, 1 teaspoon coriander seeds, 1 teaspoon fennel seeds and 1 teaspoon sugar and cook for 1–2 minutes. Add 1 kg (2¼ lb) peeled, deseeded and diced pumpkin and cook for 1 minute, stirring to coat. Pour in 1.2 litres (2 pints) hot chicken or vegetable stock and bring to the boil, then cook over a medium heat for 15 minutes until the pumpkin is very tender. Purée the soup with a hand-held blender or whizz in a blender, then return to the heat and season well. Swirl in 125 ml (4 fl oz) single cream and serve with chunks of crusty bread.

MOR-SOUP-JOL

20 Lamb, Chickpea and Cinnamon Broth

Serves 4

2 tablespoons ghee or argan oil
1 onion, finely chopped
1 garlic clove, finely chopped
1 teaspoon coriander seeds
1 teaspoon cumin seeds
2 dried red chillies
2–3 cinnamon sticks
250 g (8 oz) lean lamb, cut into
  thin strips
400 g (13 oz) can chickpeas,
  rinsed and drained
1.2 litres (2 pints) hot lamb or
  chicken stock
small bunch of flat leaf parsley,
  roughly chopped
salt and pepper
lemon wedges, to serve (optional)

- Heat the ghee or oil in a heavy-based saucepan, stir in the onion, garlic and spices and cook for 2–3 minutes until the onion begins to colour.

- Add the lamb and cook for 1–2 minutes, stirring to coat well, then add the chickpeas. Pour in the stock and bring to the boil, then cook over a medium heat for 15 minutes.

- Stir in the parsley and season. Serve the broth with lemon wedges to squeeze over, if liked.

 Quick Chickpea and Cinnamon Sauce Place a 400 g (13 oz) can chickpeas, rinsed and drained, 2 crushed garlic cloves and 1 teaspoon cumin seeds in a food processor and whizz to a thick purée. Melt 25 g (1 oz) butter in a heavy-based saucepan, stir in 200 ml (7 fl oz) double cream, a pinch of freshly grated nutmeg and 1 teaspoon ground cinnamon and bring to the boil, then remove from the heat and gently beat in the chickpea purée. Season, dust with a little cinnamon and serve with grilled lamb.

 Cinnamon Lamb, Chickpea and Tomato Soup Heat 2 tablespoons ghee in a large, heavy-based saucepan, stir in 1 finely chopped onion, 1 diced celery stick and 2 peeled and diced small carrots and cook for 3–4 minutes until they begin to colour. Add 2–3 crushed garlic cloves, 1 teaspoon cumin seeds and 225 g (7½ oz) diced lamb and cook for 2–3 minutes until lightly browned. Stir in 2 teaspoons turmeric, 1–2 teaspoons paprika, 2 teaspoons ground cinnamon, 1–2 teaspoons sugar and 2 bay leaves, then add 1 tablespoon tomato purée, a 400 g (13 oz) can chopped tomatoes, drained of juice, and a 400 g (13 oz) can chickpeas, rinsed and drained. Pour in 1.5 litres (2½ pints) hot lamb or chicken stock and bring to the boil, then cook over a medium heat for 20 minutes. Season and stir in a roughly chopped small bunch each of flat leaf parsley and coriander. Serve with lemon wedges to squeeze over.

30 Lemony Beef, Bean and Cumin Soup

Serves 4

2 tablespoons ghee, smen or argan oil

1 onion, finely chopped

2–3 garlic cloves, finely chopped

2 teaspoons cumin seeds

1 teaspoon sugar

250 g (8 oz) lean beef, diced

2 dried red chillies

2 teaspoons turmeric

1.5 litres (2½ pints) hot beef stock

400 g (13 oz) can kidney or broad beans, rinsed and drained

juice of 1 lemon

large bunch of flat leaf parsley, finely chopped

salt and pepper

lemon wedges, to serve

- Heat the ghee, smen or oil in a large, heavy-based saucepan, stir in the onion, garlic, cumin seeds and sugar and cook for 2–3 minutes until the onion begins to colour.

- Add the beef and cook for 1 minute, stirring to coat well, then add the chillies and turmeric. Pour in the stock and bring to the boil, then cook over a medium heat for 15 minutes.

- Stir in the beans, lemon juice and most of the parsley, reduce the heat and cook for a further 10 minutes. Season, garnish with the remaining parsley and serve with lemon wedges to squeeze over.

 Cumin and Lemon Beef and Beans

Heat 2 tablespoons ghee in a saucepan, stir in 1 chopped onion, 2 chopped garlic cloves, 2 teaspoons cumin seeds and 1 teaspoon sugar. Cook for 2–3 minutes. Toss in 4 slices of ready-cooked beef, cut into strips, and cook for 1–2 minutes. Add a 400 g (13 oz) can mixed beans, rinsed and drained, and cook for 1 minute, then pour in the juice of 1 lemon. Cook for 3–4 minutes, then season and stir in a finely chopped small bunch of flat leaf parsley. Serve on toasted flatbreads with dollops of yogurt.

 Beef and Cumin Seed Broth with Lemon Heat 1 tablespoon ghee, smen or argan oil in a heavy-based saucepan, stir in 1 finely chopped onion, 2 finely chopped garlic cloves, 1 teaspoon cumin seeds and 1 teaspoon sugar and cook for 2–3 minutes. Add 350 g (11½ oz) lean beef, cut into thin strips, and cook for 1 minute, stirring to coat well. Add 1 teaspoon turmeric, 1–2 dried red chillies and a bunch of parsley leaves. Pour in 1.2 litres (2 pints) hot beef or chicken stock and bring to the boil, then cook over a medium heat for 15 minutes. Season to taste. Meanwhile, melt 1 tablespoon ghee in a small frying pan, add 1 teaspoon cumin seeds and cook, stirring, for 1–2 minutes, then swirl it into the broth. Garnish with a finely chopped small bunch of flat leaf parsley and serve with lemon wedges to squeeze over.

MOR-SOUP-ZER

30 Fino, Harissa and Grilled Pepper Fish Soup

Serves 4

2 red, orange or yellow peppers
2 tablespoons olive or argan oil
1 onion, finely chopped
2 garlic cloves, finely chopped
1–2 teaspoons harissa paste
 (see page 70)
small bunch of flat leaf parsley,
 finely chopped
1 litre (1¾ pints) hot fish stock
150 ml (¼ pint) fino sherry or
 white wine
400 g (13 oz) can chopped
 tomatoes, drained of juice
900 g (2 lb) firm-fleshed fish,
 such as sea bass or haddock,
 skinned and cut into chunks
salt and pepper
small bunch of coriander, finely
 chopped, to garnish
crusty bread, to serve

- Place the peppers directly over a gas flame or under a preheated hot grill for 4–5 minutes, turning occasionally, until the skin is charred in places. Place in a plastic food bag to sweat for 5 minutes, then hold by the stalks under cold running water and carefully peel off the skins. Place on a board, remove the stalks and seeds, then cut into thick strips. Set aside.

- Meanwhile, heat the oil in a large, heavy-based saucepan, add the onion and garlic and cook for 2–3 minutes until they begin to colour. Add the harissa and parsley and pour in the stock. Bring to the boil, then reduce the heat and simmer for 10 minutes.

- Add the sherry or wine and tomatoes, then gently stir in the fish pieces and grilled peppers. Increase the heat and bring to the boil, then reduce the heat and simmer for 5–6 minutes, or until the fish is cooked through. Season, garnish with the coriander and serve with crusty bread.

---

1 Harissa Fish Stock Couscous

Place 500–700 g (1–1½ lb) heads, tails, bones and scrap pieces of fish in a saucepan. Add 2 smashed garlic cloves, 1 quartered onion, 4–6 black peppercorns, a bunch of flat leaf parsley leaves and stalks, 1 teaspoon sea salt and 1 teaspoon harissa paste (see page 70). Add 1.2 litres (2 pints) boiling water and boil for 8–10 minutes. Strain, spoon over couscous and garnish with a finely chopped small bunch of coriander.

2 Fino and Harissa Fish Broth

Heat 1–2 tablespoons olive oil in a heavy-based saucepan, add 1 finely chopped onion, 2 finely chopped garlic cloves and 1 teaspoon sugar and cook for 2–3 minutes until the onion begins to colour. Stir in 1–2 teaspoons harissa paste (see page 70), a 400 g (13 oz) can chopped tomatoes, drained of juice, 1 litre (1¾ pints) hot fish stock and 150 ml (¼ pint) fino sherry and bring to the boil, then cook over a medium heat for 10 minutes. Slide in 700 g (1½ lb) firm white fish, skinned and cut into chunks, and simmer gently for 5–6 minutes, or until cooked through. Season to taste, garnish with a finely chopped small bunch of coriander and serve with couscous or chunks of crusty bread.

MOR-SOUP-QEL

20 Mussel, Chilli and Coriander Broth

Serves 4

2 tablespoons olive oil
1 onion, finely chopped
2 garlic cloves, finely chopped
2 red chillies, deseeded and
    finely chopped
1–2 teaspoons turmeric
850 ml (1½ pints) hot fish or
    shellfish stock
300 ml (½ pint) white wine
1 kg (2¼ lb) live mussels
small bunch of flat leaf parsley,
    finely chopped
small bunch of coriander,
    finely chopped
salt and pepper
chunks of crusty bread,
    to serve

- Heat the oil in a heavy-based saucepan, add the onion, garlic and chillies and cook for 2–3 minutes. Stir in the turmeric, then pour in the stock and white wine. Bring to the boil, then reduce the heat and cook gently for 8–10 minutes.

- Meanwhile, scrub the mussels in plenty of cold water. Scrape off any barnacles and beards with a knife and discard any mussels that fail to open when lightly tapped on a work surface. Rinse well, then drain.

- Season the broth, then tip in the mussels with half the herbs and bring to the boil. Cover and cook gently for 5 minutes, or until the mussels open. Discard any that remain shut. Scatter with the remaining herbs and serve with crusty bread.

---

10 Chilli and Coriander Mussel Stock

Couscous Put 1 kg (2¼ lb) live mussels, prepared as above, into a large saucepan. Add 1 quartered onion, 2 smashed garlic cloves, 2 dried red chillies and a bunch of coriander leaves and stalks. Pour in enough water to cover, cover and bring to the boil, then cook for 6–8 minutes, or until the mussels open. Discard any that remain shut. Season and spoon over couscous.

30 Creamy Chilli and Coriander Mussel

Broth Heat 2 tablespoons olive oil in a large, heavy-based saucepan, add 1 finely chopped onion, 2 finely chopped garlic cloves and 2 deseeded and finely chopped red chillies and cook for 2–3 minutes. Add 2 teaspoons turmeric and 2 fresh or dried bay leaves, then pour in 850 ml (1½ pints) hot fish stock and 300 ml (½ pint) white wine. Bring to the boil, then reduce the heat and simmer for 10 minutes. Meanwhile, prepare 1.5 kg (3 lb) live mussels as above. Tip into the pan, cover and simmer for a further 5 minutes, or until the mussels open. Strain the liquid through a colander into a separate saucepan and simmer over a low heat. Shell the mussels, discarding the shells and any that have remained shut. Add the mussels to the broth, stir in 150 ml (¼ pint) double cream and a finely chopped small bunch of coriander and season. Garnish with a little more finely chopped coriander and serve with couscous or chunks of crusty bread.

30 Minty Chicken and Rice Soup

Serves 4

2 tablespoons olive or argan oil
2 onions, finely chopped
1 red chilli, deseeded and
   finely chopped
1 teaspoon coriander seeds
2 teaspoons dried mint
300 g (10 oz) skinless chicken
   breast fillets, cut into thin strips
100 g (3½ oz) medium grain
   white rice, such as paella,
   rinsed and drained
2 teaspoons tomato purée
1 teaspoon sugar
1.5 litres (2½ pints) hot chicken
   stock
salt and pepper
small bunch of mint, finely
   shredded, to garnish
lemon wedges, to serve (optional)

- Heat the oil in a heavy-based saucepan, stir in the onions, chilli and coriander seeds and cook for 2–3 minutes. Add the dried mint and chicken and cook for 2 minutes, stirring to coat well.

- Stir in the rice, then add the tomato purée, sugar and stock. Bring to the boil, then reduce the heat and simmer for 20–25 minutes until cooked through.

- Season, garnish with the shredded mint and serve with lemon wedges to squeeze over, if liked.

 Quick Chicken and Mint Stock Couscous In a small saucepan, stir 1 chicken stock cube into 600 ml (1 pint) boiling water until it dissolves. Add the juice of 1 lemon, 2 dried red chillies and a large bunch of mint leaves. Bring to the boil and cook over a medium heat for 5–6 minutes. Season and spoon over couscous.

 Chicken and Mint Broth Heat 1 tablespoon olive oil in a heavy-based saucepan, add 1 finely chopped onion, 2 finely chopped garlic cloves, 1 deseeded and chopped green chilli and 1 teaspoon coriander seeds and cook for 1–2 minutes. Stir in 2 teaspoons dried mint and 300 g (10 oz) thinly sliced skinless chicken breast fillets and cook for 1–2 minutes. Pour in 1 litre (1¾ pints) hot chicken stock and bring to the boil, then cook over a medium heat for 15 minutes until cooked through. Season and stir in a finely chopped small bunch of mint. Serve with lemon wedges to squeeze over.

10 Simple Herb, Chilli and Saffron Broth

Serves 4

850 ml (1½ pints) boiling water
2–3 dried red chillies
2 teaspoons cumin seeds
1 teaspoon coriander seeds
1 teaspoon saffron threads
small bunch of flat leaf parsley
   leaves and stalks
small bunch of coriander leaves
   and stalks
small bunch of mint leaves
4–6 peppercorns
1 teaspoon sea salt

- Pour the measurement water into a saucepan set over a medium heat. Add the remaining ingredients and boil gently for 8–10 minutes.

- Strain and serve between courses, or as a digestive.

 20 Herby Vegetable Soup with Chillies

Heat 2 tablespoons olive oil in a heavy-based saucepan, add 1 chopped onion, 2 chopped garlic cloves and 1 teaspoon each of coriander seeds and cumin seeds and cook for 1–2 minutes. Stir in 2 diced celery sticks, 2 peeled and diced carrots, 3 peeled and diced potatoes and 850 ml (1½ pints) hot chicken or vegetable stock and bring to the boil. Add 225 g (7½ oz) baby spinach leaves and a bunch of flat leaf parsley leaves and stalks, then cook over a medium heat for 12–15 minutes. Purée with a hand-held blender or whizz in a blender. Return to the heat and season. Serve garnished with 1–2 deseeded and finely chopped red or green chillies.

 30 Herb, Chilli and Saffron Vegetable Soup Heat 2 tablespoons olive or argan oil in a heavy-based saucepan, add 2 finely chopped onions, 2 finely chopped garlic cloves, 2 deseeded and finely chopped red or green chillies and 1 teaspoon each of cumin seeds and coriander seeds and cook for 2–3 minutes. Add 2 diced celery sticks, 2 peeled and diced carrots and 4 peeled and diced new potatoes, then cover and cook for 2–3 minutes. Stir in 2 diced courgettes, a pinch of saffron threads and 1.5 litres (2½ pints) hot vegetable or chicken stock. Bring to the boil, then reduce the heat and cook gently for 20 minutes. Season and stir in a finely chopped small bunch each of flat leaf parsley,

coriander and mint leaves and a few finely chopped dill sprigs. Garnish with a little more finely chopped dill and serve with lemon wedges to squeeze over.

MOR-SOUP-KEQ

30 Carrot, Coriander and Lentil Soup

Serves 4

2 tablespoons ghee or argan oil
1 onion, finely chopped
25 g (1 oz) root ginger, chopped
2–3 garlic cloves, finely chopped
2 teaspoons coriander seeds
1 teaspoon cumin seeds
1 teaspoon sugar
4 carrots, peeled and diced
150 g (5 oz) brown lentils, rinsed
1–2 teaspoons ras el hanout
400 g (13 oz) can chopped
    tomatoes, drained of juice
1.2 litres (2 pints) hot chicken stock
bunch of coriander, finely chopped
salt and pepper

To serve

3–4 tablespoons natural yogurt
crusty bread

- Heat the ghee or oil in a heavy-based saucepan, stir in the onion, ginger, garlic, seeds and sugar and cook for 2–3 minutes. Add the carrots and cook for 2 minutes, stirring to coat well. Stir in the lentils, ras el hanout, tomatoes and stock and bring to the boil, then reduce the heat and cook gently for 20 minutes.

- Season, stir in most of the chopped coriander and cook for a further 5 minutes until the carrots and lentils are tender. Swirl a little of the yogurt into the soup, then serve garnished with the remaining coriander, with dollops of yogurt and crusty bread.

 Lentils with Carrot and Coriander Soup

Heat 1–2 tablespoons ghee in a saucepan, stir in 1 chopped onion, 2 chopped garlic cloves, 1 tablespoon chopped root ginger, 2 teaspoons dried red chilli, 2 teaspoons coriander seeds and 1 teaspoon sugar and cook for 3–4 minutes. Add a 400 g (13 oz) can brown lentils and heat through. Season and stir in 2 tablespoons chopped coriander. Meanwhile, heat through 2 x 600 g (1¼ lb) pots carrot and coriander soup. Top with the lentils and dollops of natural yogurt.

 Puréed Carrot and Coriander Soup

Heat 2 tablespoons ghee in a heavy-based saucepan, stir in 1 finely chopped onion, 2 finely chopped garlic cloves, 25 g (1 oz) peeled and finely chopped fresh root ginger, 2 teaspoons coriander seeds and 1 teaspoon sugar and cook for 2–3 minutes. Add 1 kg (2¼ lb) peeled and diced carrots, 1 teaspoon ras el hanout, a small bunch of coriander leaves and stalks and 850 ml (1½ pints) hot chicken or vegetable stock and bring to the boil, then cook over a medium heat for 15 minutes until the carrots are tender. Purée the soup with a hand-held blender or whizz in a blender. Return to the heat and season, then serve with dollops of natural yogurt, garnished with a little more finely chopped coriander.

10 Chilled Almond and Garlic Soup

Serves 4

150 g (5 oz) blanched almonds, roughly chopped

3–4 slices of stale white bread, crusts removed

4 garlic cloves, roughly chopped

4 tablespoons olive oil, plus extra to garnish

850 ml (1½ pints) chilled water or chicken stock

1–2 tablespoons white wine or apple vinegar

salt

To serve

ice cubes

seedless green grapes, sliced

1 red or green chilli, deseeded and finely sliced

- Put the blanched almonds into a food processor and whizz to a paste. Add the bread and garlic and replace the lid. With the motor running, drizzle in the oil through the feed tube, then gradually pour in the water or stock until the mixture has a smooth pouring consistency. Add the vinegar and season with salt.

- Place 2–3 ice cubes in each of 4 serving bowls, ladle over the soup and serve sprinkled with the grapes and chilli and drizzled with olive oil.

 Garlic, Almond and Chorizo Soup

Heat 2 tablespoons olive oil in a saucepan, stir in 1 chopped onion, 3–4 chopped garlic cloves, 1 deseeded and chopped red chilli and 2 teaspoons fennel seeds and cook for 2–3 minutes. Add 350 g (11½ oz) sliced chorizo and cook for 1–2 minutes, then stir in 1 tablespoon tomato purée, 1–2 tablespoons ground almonds, 700 ml (1¼ pints) hot chicken stock and 150 ml (¼ pint) white wine and bring to the boil. Reduce the heat and simmer for 15 minutes. Season and serve garnished with coriander.

 Garlicky Chorizo and Potato Soup with Toasted Almonds

Dry-fry 2–3 tablespoons blanched almonds in a small, heavy-based frying pan over a medium heat for 3–4 minutes until they turn golden brown and emit a nutty aroma. Using a pestle and mortar, coarsely grind the almonds. Set aside. Heat 2 tablespoons olive or argan oil in a heavy-based saucepan, stir in 1 finely chopped onion and 1 deseeded and finely chopped red chilli and cook for 2–3 minutes. Add 250 g (8 oz) thinly sliced chorizo and cook for 2 minutes, then stir in 4 crushed garlic cloves and 1–2 teaspoons smoked paprika. Add 700 g (1½ lb) peeled and diced new potatoes and mix well, then pour in 150 ml (¼ pint) white wine and 850 ml (1½ pints) hot chicken stock. Bring to the boil, then cook over a medium heat for 15–20 minutes until the potatoes are tender. Season and stir in a finely chopped small bunch of flat leaf parsley. Scatter over the almonds and garnish with a little more finely chopped parsley.

MOR-SOUP-LEA

30 Apple and Butternut Soup with Chilli Oil

Serves 4

3 green apples
1–2 tablespoons olive or argan oil
20 g (¾ oz) butter
1 onion, finely chopped
25 g (1 oz) fresh root ginger,
   peeled and finely chopped
2 teaspoons fennel seeds
1 teaspoon coriander seeds
1 teaspoon cumin seeds
1 teaspoon sugar
1 small butternut squash, about
   900 g (2 lb), peeled, deseeded
   and diced
1 litre (1¾ pints) hot chicken stock
150 ml (¼ pint) double cream
salt and pepper
chilli oil, for drizzling

- Core and very finely slice 1 of the apples horizontally to form thin discs. Place on a wire rack set over a baking sheet and bake in a preheated oven, 150°C (300°F), Gas Mark 2, for 20–25 minutes. Peel, core and dice the remaining apples.

- Meanwhile, heat the oil and butter in a heavy-based saucepan, stir in the onion, ginger, seeds and sugar and cook for 1–2 minutes. Add the squash and cook for 2–3 minutes, stirring to coat well. Add the diced apples and stock and bring to the boil, then cook over a medium heat for 20 minutes.

- Stir in the cream and season. Ladle into 4 serving bowls, add baked apple slices to each and drizzle over a little chilli oil.

10 Apple Purée with Chilli Oil

Place 300 g (10 oz) shop-bought chilled apple purée, the juice of 1 lemon, 2 tablespoons orange blossom water and a finely chopped small bunch each of mint and coriander in a bowl. Season with a little salt and pepper and add a little sugar or honey, if necessary. Spoon the mixture into a bowl and serve with a drizzle of chilli oil as an appetizer or a sauce for grilled meat.

20 Puréed Apple Soup with Chilli Oil

Heat 2 tablespoons olive oil and a knob of butter in a heavy-based saucepan, stir in 1 finely chopped onion, 2 finely chopped garlic cloves, 2 teaspoons fennel seeds and 1–2 teaspoons sugar and cook for 2–3 minutes. Add 5–6 peeled, cored and diced apples and 850 ml (1½ pints) hot chicken or vegetable stock and bring to the boil, then cook over a medium heat for 12–15 minutes until the apple is soft. Purée the soup with a hand-held blender or whizz in a blender. Return to the heat, season and add a little more sugar if the apples are very tart. Drizzle over a little chilli oil and serve as an appetizer or between courses.

MOR-SOUP-GOD

Chilli and Fino Gazpacho

Serves 4

6 tomatoes
1 small cucumber, peeled, deseeded and diced
1 red pepper, deseeded and diced
1 onion, finely chopped
2 red or green chillies, deseeded and finely chopped
2 garlic cloves, crushed
2 tablespoons olive oil
juice of 1 lemon
1 teaspoon Tabasco sauce
700 ml (1¼ pints) chilled tomato juice
50 ml (2 fl oz) fino sherry
1–2 teaspoons sugar
salt and pepper

To serve

ice cubes (optional)
3–4 tablespoons natural yogurt
small bunch of coriander, finely chopped

- Place the tomatoes in a heatproof bowl and pour over boiling water to cover. Leave for 1–2 minutes, then drain, cut a cross at the stem end of each tomato and peel off the skins. Cut into quarters, remove the seeds and finely dice the flesh.

- Put the tomatoes into a bowl with the cucumber, red pepper, onion, chillies and garlic. Add the oil, lemon juice and Tabasco and mix well. Put a third of the mixture into a food processor with half the tomato juice and whizz to a purée. Return to the bowl and combine with the remaining tomato juice and the sherry. Season with salt and pepper and add sugar to taste. Cover and chill for at least 15 minutes.

- Spoon the gazpacho into 4 serving bowls, adding an ice cube to each if not sufficiently chilled. Serve with dollops of yogurt and sprinkled with the coriander.

Gazpacho with Herb and Chilli Relish

Finely chop a large bunch of coriander and a small bunch of mint and place in a bowl. Add 2 finely chopped and deseeded green chillies and 1 teaspoon sea salt and mix well. Stir half the relish into 600 ml (1 pint) shop-bought chilled gazpacho. Put some crushed ice into 2 glasses, pour over the soup and sprinkle with the remaining relish.

 ### Quick Chilli and Fino Gazpacho

Peel, deseed and roughly chop 1 small cucumber and place in a food processor. Roughly chop 1 onion, 1 deseeded red or green pepper, 2 deseeded red or green chillies and 2 garlic cloves and add to the processor with 1 tablespoon tomato purée, 1–2 teaspoons sugar, 2 tablespoons olive oil and the juice of 1 lemon. Whizz to a thick purée, then gradually pour in 600 ml (1 pint) chilled tomato juice and 50 ml (2 fl oz) fino sherry and season to taste. Cover and chill for at least 10 minutes, or serve with ice cubes. Garnish with a small bunch of coriander, finely chopped, and serve with a glass of fino sherry.

MOR-SOUP-TIY

Chicken, Nut and Cinnamon Pie

Serves 4

2–3 tablespoons olive oil
100 g (3½ oz) butter
3 onions, finely sliced
2 garlic cloves, finely chopped
2 teaspoons coriander seeds
2–3 tablespoons blanched
   almonds, chopped
3 teaspoons ground cinnamon
1 teaspoon ground ginger
1 teaspoon paprika
300 g (10 oz) skinless chicken
   breast fillets, cut into chunks
1–2 tablespoons orange
   blossom water
small bunch of flat leaf parsley,
   finely chopped
small bunch of coriander,
   finely chopped
7–8 sheets of filo pastry
1 egg yolk mixed with a little water
salt and pepper
2 teaspoons icing sugar, for dusting

- Heat the oil and a knob of the butter in a heavy-based frying pan, stir in the onions, garlic and coriander seeds and cook for 2–3 minutes. Stir in the almonds, 2 teaspoons ground cinnamon, the ground ginger and paprika, then add the chicken and coat well. Add the orange blossom water, reduce the heat and cook gently for 3–4 minutes until almost dry. Toss in the herbs and season.

- Melt the remaining butter in a small saucepan. Separate the sheets of filo and place under a clean, damp tea towel to prevent them drying out. Brush a little butter over the base of a round ovenproof dish and cover with 1 sheet of filo, flopping the sides over the edge. Brush with butter and place another sheet on top. Repeat with another 2 layers. Spread over the chicken mixture, then fold over the edges. Cover with the remaining filo, brushing with butter. Tuck the overlapping edges under the pie, then brush with the egg wash.

- Bake in a preheated oven, 200°C (400°F), Gas Mark 6, for about 20 minutes until the pastry is puffed and golden. Dust with the remaining ground cinnamon, followed by the icing sugar.

 Simple Chicken, Nut and Cinnamon Wraps Place 4 tortilla wraps on a flat surface and fill with 225 g (7½ oz) shop-bought ready-cooked chicken, cut into thin strips, sliced onion, a sprinkling of chopped mixed nuts, roughly chopped flat leaf parsley and coriander, dollops of thick natural yogurt and a little harissa paste. Roll up and dust with cinnamon to serve.

 Warm Chicken, Nut and Cinnamon Wraps Heat 2 tablespoons oil in a heavy-based frying pan, stir in 1 finely chopped onion, 2 finely chopped garlic cloves, 1 tablespoon peeled and finely chopped fresh root ginger and 2 teaspoons coriander seeds and cook for 2–3 minutes. Add 300 g (10 oz) finely sliced skinless chicken breast fillet and cook for 2–3 minutes, then stir in 1–2 teaspoons ground cinnamon, 1 teaspoon paprika and 2 tablespoons mixed chopped nuts. Season, cover and cook gently for 3–4 minutes. Place 4 warmed tortilla wraps on a flat surface, drizzle over a little chilli oil or smear with a little harissa paste (see page 70), then sprinkle with chopped coriander. Spoon over the chicken mixture, then roll up. Serve with spicy dips, pickles or chutneys.

Feta, Olive and Preserved Lemon Pastries

Serves 4

175 g (6 oz) shop-bought chilled
  ready-made puff pastry

flour, for dusting

olive oil, for brushing

175 g (6 oz) feta cheese,
  crumbled

2 tablespoons pitted black olives,
  finely chopped

finely chopped rind of 1 preserved
  lemon (see page 68)

2 teaspoons dried mint

- Roll out the pastry on a lightly floured surface to a rectangle about 5 mm (¼ inch) thick, then cut into 8 thin strips. Place them on lightly oiled baking sheets and brush each strip with a little oil.

- In a small bowl, gently mix together the feta, olives, preserved lemon rind and half the mint. Scatter a thin layer of the mixture over each pastry strip, then place in a preheated oven, 200°C (400°F), Gas Mark 6, for 12–15 minutes until the pastry is cooked. Sprinkle the remaining mint over the tops and serve hot.

 Feta, Olive and Preserved Lemon Toasted Pittas Lightly toast 4 pitta breads or other flatbreads. Melt 1–2 tablespoons butter or ghee in a small saucepan and brush a little over each bread. Scatter over 175 g (6 oz) crumbled feta cheese, 2 tablespoons pitted and chopped black olives and the finely chopped rind of 1 preserved lemon (see page 68) and serve sprinkled with mint and flat leaf parsley leaves.

 Feta, Olive and Preserved Lemon Pastry Roll Roll out 175 g (6 oz) shop-bought chilled ready-made puff pastry on a lightly floured surface to a rectangle about 3–4 mm (¹/₆ inch) thick. In a bowl, mix together 175 g (6 oz) crumbled feta cheese, 2 tablespoons pitted and finely chopped black olives, the finely chopped rind of 1 preserved lemon (see page 68) and a finely chopped small bunch each of mint and flat leaf parsley, then add 1 egg and mix well. Spoon the mixture along a long edge of the pastry. Roll the edge over the mixture, fold over the short edges and roll up the pastry so that it resembles a long, stuffed log. Place on a lightly oiled baking sheet and brush with a little olive oil. Using a sharp knife, carefully make several short slashes on the top of the pastry. Place in a preheated oven, 200°C (400°F), Gas Mark 6, for 20–25 minutes until cooked and browned.

20 Deep-Fried Fish and Chermoula Pastries

Serves 4

450 g (14½ oz) skinless cod or
haddock fillets, boned and cut
into bite-sized pieces
200 g (7 oz) filo pastry, cut into
10 cm (4 inch) squares
50 g (2 oz) butter, melted
sunflower oil, for deep-frying
salt and pepper
chilli dipping sauce, to serve

For the chermoula

2 tablespoons olive oil
juice of 1 lemon
1 teaspoon ground cumin
1 teaspoon smoked paprika
1 red chilli, deseeded and chopped
finely chopped rind of ½ preserved
lemon (see page 68)
2 garlic cloves, crushed
1 tablespoon chopped coriander
1 tablespoon chopped parsley

- Mix together all the chermoula ingredients in a bowl. Toss in the fish pieces and season well.

- Lay out the filo under a clean, damp tea towel to prevent it drying out. Place 1 filo square on a flat surface and brush it with a little melted butter, then put another on top at an angle and brush it with more butter. Repeat with a third sheet at an angle. Place a small spoonful of the fish in the centre and carefully pull up the edges, pinching the ends together using wet fingertips. Repeat with the remaining ingredients to make 16–20 pastries.

- In a large, deep saucepan, heat enough oil for deep-frying to 180–190°C (350–375°F), or until a cube of bread browns in 30 seconds. Deep-fry the pastries in batches for 2–3 minutes until lightly golden. Remove with a slotted spoon and drain on kitchen paper. Serve hot with a drizzle of chilli oil, a little harissa paste or a dipping sauce.

 Chermoula Fish Toasts

Brush 4 boned skinless cod or haddock fillets with olive oil and season. Cook under a preheated medium grill for 2–3 minutes on each side until cooked through. Meanwhile, toast 4 flatbreads and drizzle with olive oil. Place the fish on the toasts and drizzle over 1 tablespoon ready-made chermoula paste. Sprinkle with the chopped rind of ½ preserved lemon (see page 68) and serve.

 Baked Fish and Chermoula Pastries

Toss 450 g (14½ oz) skinless cod or haddock fillets, boned and cut into bite-sized chunks, in 2 tablespoons ready-made chermoula paste and season well. Lay out 8 sheets of filo pastry under a clean, damp tea towel to prevent them drying out. Place 1 sheet on a flat surface and brush the top with a little olive or sunflower oil, then put 1/8 of the fish mixture in the centre. Fold over 2 sides to enclose the filling, then pull over the other sides to form a square parcel. Brush the edges with a little water and stick together. Repeat with the remaining ingredients. Place the parcels, seam side down, in a lightly oiled baking dish. Brush with a little more oil and place in a preheated oven, 200°C (400°F), Gas Mark 6, for 20 minutes until crisp and golden brown.

Mini Lamb and Harissa Pizzas

Serves 4

175 g (6 oz) lean minced lamb
1 onion, finely chopped
2 garlic cloves, crushed
2 teaspoons cumin seeds
1 teaspoon ground coriander
1 teaspoon ground fenugreek
1–2 teaspoons harissa paste
   (see page 70)
1 tablespoon olive oil, plus extra
   for greasing
4 shop-bought ready-made mini
   pizza bases
2 teaspoons tomato purée
small bunch of coriander, finely
   chopped
salt and pepper

- Mix together the lamb, onion, garlic, spices and harissa in a bowl. Add the oil, mix well and season, then knead to a sticky paste.

- Place the pizza bases on a lightly oiled baking sheet and lightly smear with the tomato purée, then spread a thin layer of the meat mixture over each.

- Place in a preheated oven, 220°C (425°F), Gas Mark 7, for 12–15 minutes. Scatter the chopped coriander over the tops and serve hot.

 ### Lamb and Harissa Toasts

Heat 2 tablespoons olive oil in a frying pan, stir in 1 chopped onion, 2 chopped garlic cloves, 1 teaspoon each of cumin seeds and sugar and cook for 2 minutes. Stir in 1–2 teaspoons harissa paste (see page 70) and 225 g (7½ oz) minced lamb and cook, stirring, for 5–6 minutes. Season and toss in a finely chopped small bunch of coriander. Meanwhile, toast 4 slices of crusty loaf and drizzle with a little olive oil. Spoon over the lamb, garnish with a little more coriander and serve with dollops of natural yogurt, pickles or chutney.

 ### Lamb and Harissa Rolls

Using a large pestle and mortar, pound 350 g (11½ oz) lean minced lamb with 2 crushed garlic cloves, 2 teaspoons ground cumin, 1 teaspoon ground coriander, 1 teaspoon ground fenugreek and 2 teaspoons harissa paste (see page 70). Alternatively, whizz together in a food processor. Mix in a finely chopped small bunch of flat leaf parsley and 1 tablespoon olive oil to make a smooth paste, then season. Roll out a 500 g (l lb) pack of shop-bought chilled ready-made puff pastry on a lightly floured surface to about 40 x 18 cm (16 x 7 inches). Spread over the meat paste in a thin layer, taking it right to the edges. Starting from a long edge, roll up the pastry into a log. Using a sharp knife, slice into bite-sized portions and place on a lightly oiled baking sheet. Bake in a preheated oven, 200°C (400°F), Gas Mark 6, for 15–20 minutes until puffed and golden. Serve hot with chilli dipping sauce and chutneys.

MOR-SOUP-WUQ

Chorizo and Parsley Eggs

Serves 4

1 tablespoon ghee or butter
450 g (14½ oz) chorizo or
  merguez sausage, thinly sliced
  diagonally
8 eggs
large bunch of flat leaf parsley,
  roughly chopped
salt and pepper

- Heat the ghee or butter in a large, heavy-based frying pan, stir in the sausage and cook for 2–3 minutes.

- Break the eggs into the pan, cover and cook over a medium heat for 4–5 minutes until the whites are firm. Season, scatter over the parsley and serve hot.

 Quick Potato and Parsley Omelette

Put 450 g (14½ oz) canned new potatoes into a bowl and mash them to a coarse paste. In a bowl, beat together 8 eggs and 150 ml (¼ pint) milk, then stir in 1 tablespoon finely chopped flat leaf parsley and 1 teaspoon smoked paprika. Season well and beat in the mashed potato. Heat 1–2 tablespoons ghee or butter in a flameproof, heavy-based frying pan, tip in the potato mixture, cover and cook gently for 8–10 minutes until firm. Take off the lid, dot with a little butter and place under a preheated medium grill for 3–4 minutes until browned. Divide into 4 and garnish with a little more finely chopped parsley.

 Potato, Chorizo and Parsley Omelette Cook 4–5 new potatoes in a saucepan of boiling water for 8–10 minutes, or until tender. Drain, refresh under cold running water and drain again, then peel off the skins and cut into thin slices. In a bowl, beat together 8 eggs and 300 ml (½ pint) milk, then stir in 2 tablespoons finely chopped flat leaf parsley and season. Heat 1–2 tablespoons ghee or butter in a heavy-based frying pan, stir in 1 teaspoon cumin seeds and 1 teaspoon fennel seeds and cook for 1–2 minutes. Add 250 g (8 oz) thinly sliced chorizo and cook for 1–2 minutes, then add the potatoes, coat well and cook for a further 1–2 minutes. Pour in the egg mixture, cover and cook over a low heat for 10–12 minutes, moving the mixture occasionally, until firm. Turn off the heat and leave to stand, still covered, for a few minutes. Divide into 4 and garnish with a little more finely chopped parsley or coriander.

30 Courgette, Mint and Bread Omelette

Serves 4–6

2 courgettes, thinly sliced
2 tablespoons olive oil
50 g (2 oz) butter
1 onion, sliced
small bunch of mint, roughly
  chopped
6 eggs
2 slices of white bread, crusts
  removed, soaked in a little milk
salt and pepper
1 scant teaspoon paprika,
  for dusting

- Place the courgettes in a colander and sprinkle with a little salt to draw out the juices. Leave to stand for about 5 minutes, then rinse and pat dry.

- Heat the oil and a little of the butter in a heavy-based frying pan, stir in the onion and cook for 2–3 minutes until softened. Add the courgettes and cook for a further 3–4 minutes until golden. Toss in the mint and leave to cool slightly.

- Beat the eggs lightly in a bowl. Squeeze the bread dry and add to the eggs, crumbling it with your fingers. Beat well, season and stir in the cooled courgette mixture.

- Melt the remaining butter in the frying pan, tip in the egg mixture, cover and cook gently for 10–15 minutes until set. Dust with the paprika, then cut diagonally into diamond shapes and serve.

---

10 Herby Courgette Eggs

Heat 2 tablespoons olive oil and a knob of butter in a heavy-based frying pan, stir in 1 sliced courgette and cook for 3–4 minutes until it begins to colour. Toss in a finely chopped small bunch each of mint, dill and flat leaf parsley, then make 4 wells in the mixture. Break 4 eggs into the wells, cover and cook for 4–5 minutes until the whites are firm. Season to taste, garnish with a little more finely chopped mint and dill and serve immediately.

20 Herb and Bread Omelette

Soak 2 slices of white bread in a little milk for 2–3 minutes. Lightly beat 6 eggs in a bowl. Squeeze the bread dry and crumble it with your fingers into the eggs. Add a roughly chopped small bunch each of flat leaf parsley and mint and several roughly chopped dill sprigs. Season well and mix thoroughly. Heat 2 tablespoons olive oil in a heavy-based frying pan, tip in the egg mixture, cover and cook gently for 10–15 minutes until set. Dust with a little paprika, then cut into 4 and serve.

MOR-SOUP-RIO

Chilli and Herb Sweet Potato Pancakes

Serves 4

150 g (5 oz) plain flour
3 eggs, lightly beaten
125 ml (4 fl oz) milk
1 tablespoon olive oil
350 g (11½ oz) sweet potatoes, peeled and roughly grated
2 onions, finely sliced
1 red or green chilli, deseeded and finely sliced
4–6 sage leaves, finely chopped
1 tablespoon thyme leaves
sunflower oil, for frying
salt and pepper
sumac, for sprinkling (optional)

- Sift the flour into a bowl, make a well in the centre and pour in the eggs. Gradually add the milk, beating continuously to form a smooth batter. Beat in the olive oil. Add the sweet potatoes, onions, chilli, sage and thyme, season well with salt and pepper and mix thoroughly.

- Heat a little sunflower oil in a frying pan, swirling it evenly over the base. When hot, pour in 3–4 small ladlefuls of the batter and press each flat. Cook for 2–3 minutes on each side until golden brown, then drain on kitchen paper. Repeat with the remaining batter to make 6–8 pancakes. Serve sprinkled with sea salt or sumac.

Sweet Potato Crisps with Chilli and Herb Honey Peel and finely slice 1 sweet potato. In a deep saucepan, heat enough sunflower oil for deep-frying to 180–190°C (350–375°F), or until a cube of bread browns in 30 seconds. Deep-fry the sweet potatoes in batches for 2–3 minutes until lightly brown. Meanwhile, heat together 2–3 tablespoons honey, 1 tablespoon finely crumbled dried sage and 1 teaspoon finely chopped dried red chilli in a small saucepan. Remove the crisps with a slotted spoon and drain on kitchen paper. Tip on to a plate, drizzle over the sage honey and serve.

 Sweet Potato, Chilli and Herb Pancakes Sift 4 tablespoons plain flour and a pinch of salt into a bowl, make a well in the centre and pour in 1 lightly beaten egg. Gradually beat in 150 ml (¼ pint) milk to form a smooth batter. Add a few drops of olive oil, 150 g (5 oz) peeled and coarsely grated sweet potatoes, 1–2 teaspoons finely chopped dried red chilli and 1 tablespoon each of dried thyme and finely crumbled dried sage and mix well. Cover and leave to stand for 10 minutes. Heat a nonstick pancake pan, wipe it with a little sunflower oil and add a ladleful of the batter, swirling it around to form a thin layer.

Cook for 1–2 minutes on each side until golden brown. Tip on to a plate and keep warm. Repeat with the remaining batter to make about 4 pancakes, adding a little more oil if necessary. Meanwhile, heat 2–3 tablespoons honey in a small pan. Roll up the pancakes, drizzle over a little honey and serve.

Soft-Boiled Eggs with Harissa

Serves 4

4 eggs
4 slices of bread
4 heaped teaspoons harissa paste
(see page 70)

- Place the eggs in a saucepan of water, bring to the boil and cook for 3–5 minutes, depending on how you like your eggs. Meanwhile, toast the bread and cut into long strips.

- Drain the eggs, cut them in half and serve on a plate with the strips of toast and a small bowl of harissa. To eat, first dip the strips of toast into the harissa, then dip into the egg.

 Spiced Fried Eggs with Harissa Toast

Dry-fry 2 teaspoons cumin seeds in a small, heavy-based frying pan over a medium heat for 2 minutes until they emit a nutty aroma. Break 8 eggs into a bowl without beating. Heat 1–2 tablespoons ghee or smen in a heavy-based frying pan, stir in 2–3 crushed garlic cloves and cook for 1–2 minutes until it begins to colour. Stir in the toasted seeds for 1 minute, then slide in the eggs. Sprinkle 1 teaspoon each of sea salt and dried mint over the eggs, cover and cook over a low heat for 5 minutes, or until set. Toast 4 flatbreads or 4 slices of bread, then spread a thin layer of harissa paste (see page 70) over each. Divide the eggs into 4 and lift onto the toast. Serve immediately with a little more harissa, if liked.

 Spiced Hard-Boiled Eggs with Harissa

Bring a saucepan of water to the boil, carefully lower in 4–8 eggs and bring back to the boil, then cook for 8–10 minutes. Meanwhile, dry-fry 2 teaspoons cumin seeds and 1 teaspoon coriander seeds in a small, heavy-based frying pan over a medium heat for 2 minutes until they emit a nutty aroma. Using a pestle and mortar or spice grinder, coarsely grind the spices. Drain the eggs and refresh under cold running water, then shell. Heat 1–2 tablespoons ghee, smen or argan oil in a heavy-based frying pan, stir in 2 crushed garlic cloves and cook for 1–2 minutes. Add the crushed spices and cook for 1 minute, then add the eggs, rolling them in the garlic and spices. Cover and cook over a low heat for 10 minutes, rolling the eggs occasionally. Dust the eggs with a little cinnamon and serve with a small bowl of harissa paste (see page 70) for dipping.

20 Chilli, Lime and Coriander Dried Fruit and Nuts

Serves 4

120 g (4 oz) whole almonds
2 tablespoons ghee or smen
2 tablespoons macadamia nuts, halved
2 tablespoons cashew nuts, halved
120 g (4 oz) ready-to-eat dried apricots
120 g (4 oz) ready-to-eat pitted dates
1–2 teaspoons finely chopped dried red chilli
grated rind of 1 lime
small bunch of coriander, finely chopped
salt

· Put the almonds into a bowl and pour over enough boiling water to cover. Leave for 5 minutes, then drain, refresh under cold running water and drain again. Using your fingers, rub the skins off the almonds and cut in half.

· Heat the ghee or smen in a large, heavy-based frying pan, add the nuts and dried fruit and cook, stirring, for 4–5 minutes until the nuts begin to colour. Toss in the chilli and lime rind and cook for a further 2–3 minutes, then season with salt and add the coriander. Serve immediately.

1 Chilli Oil and Coriander Mixed

Nuts Heat 2 tablespoons chilli oil in a heavy-based pan. Add 250–350 g (8–11½ oz) mixed nuts, such as almonds, cashews, macadamia and hazelnuts, and cook until they begin to colour. Season with salt to taste and toss in 1 tablespoon finely chopped coriander. Tip into a bowl and serve.

30 Nut-Stuffed Dates with Chilli Oil and

Coriander Place 225 g (7½ oz) ground almonds or pistachio nuts, 120 g (4 oz) sifted icing sugar, 1 teaspoon ground cumin, 1 beaten egg and 1–2 teaspoons lemon juice in a bowl. Using your fingers, mix together to form a sticky paste, then tip onto a surface lightly dusted with icing sugar and knead until smooth.

Shape small pieces of the paste into oblongs, then stuff into 12–16 ready-to-eat pitted dates. Heat 2 tablespoons chilli oil in a heavy-based frying pan, add the dates, stuffed side up, cover and cook over a medium heat for 4–5 minutes until heated through. Season with salt and stir in a finely chopped small bunch of coriander.

MOR-SOUP-KYA

30 Parsnip and Beetroot Crisps with Homemade Dukkah

Serves 4

sunflower or vegetable oil,
  for deep-frying
2 parsnips, peeled, halved and
  thinly sliced lengthways
2–3 raw beetroot, peeled and
  thinly sliced
salt and pepper

For the spice mix

1 tablespoon hazelnuts
1 tablespoon sesame seeds
2 teaspoons cumin seeds
2 teaspoons coriander seeds
2 teaspoons dried mint

- To make the spice mix, dry-fry the hazelnuts and seeds in a small, heavy-based frying pan over a medium heat for 2–3 minutes until they emit a nutty aroma. Using a pestle and mortar, pound the nuts and seeds to a coarse powder, or tip into a spice grinder and grind to a fine powder. Stir in the mint and season well. Set aside.

- In a deep saucepan, heat enough oil for deep-frying to 180–190°C (350–375°F), or until a cube of bread browns in 30 seconds. Deep-fry the parsnips in batches until lightly golden. Remove with a slotted spoon and drain on kitchen paper, then tip all the parsnips into a bowl while hot and sprinkle over half the dukkah spice mix.

- Reduce the heat (the beetroot slices burn easily) and deep-fry the beetroot in batches. Remove and drain as above, then tip into a bowl and sprinkle with the remaining spice mix. Serve the parsnip and beetroot crisps separately, or mixed together.

---

1 Fried Bread and Dukkah Bites

Remove the crusts of 4–8 slices of stale bread and cut them into bite-sized squares. Heat enough oil for deep-frying as above. Deep-fry the bread in batches until golden brown. Remove with a slotted spoon and drain on kitchen paper, then tip into a bowl while hot and toss with 1–2 tablespoons ready-made dukkah spice mix (for homemade, see above). Add salt or dried mint to taste and serve.

2 Baked Cheese and Dukkah Crisps

Place 150 g (5 oz) butter, 200 g (7 oz) grated Cheddar cheese (or a firm sheep's cheese), 225 g (7½ oz) plain flour, 1 egg yolk and 1 teaspoon ground cumin in a food processor and season. Pulse together until the mixture resembles coarse breadcrumbs. Roll a little of the mixture into a small ball, then flatten in the palm of your hand. Place on a baking sheet lined with greaseproof paper (you may need 2 sheets). Repeat with the remaining mixture to make about 20–30. Place in a preheated oven, 180°C (350°F), Gas Mark 4, for 10 minutes until lightly golden and slightly puffed. Meanwhile, mix together 1 tablespoon dukkah spice mix (for homemade, see above), 1 teaspoon paprika and 1 teaspoon dried mint (if not already in the mix), then sprinkle over the cheese crisps. Leave to cool and firm up on the sheets before serving.

Popcorn with Chilli Oil

Serves 4

1–2 tablespoons chilli oil,
  plus extra for drizzling
200 g (7 oz) popping corn
1 teaspoon sea salt

- Pour a thin layer of chilli oil into a heavy-based saucepan. Add enough corn to form a single layer in the pan – the quantity of oil and corn will vary according to the size of your pan. Cover with a lid and place over a medium heat, shaking the pan occasionally as the corn pops.

- When the popping stops, remove the lid and toss in a little salt to taste. Tip the popcorn into a bowl, finish with an extra drizzle of chilli oil and serve.

Popcorn with Chilli Honey

Place 3–4 tablespoons honey and 2 teaspoons finely chopped dried red chilli or 2–3 whole dried red chillies in a small saucepan and heat until the honey begins to bubble. Turn off the heat and leave to stand for 10 minutes to let the flavours mingle. Pour a thin layer of sunflower or vegetable oil into a large, heavy-based saucepan. Add enough popping corn to form a single layer in the pan. Cover with a lid and place over a medium heat, shaking the pan occasionally as the corn pops. When the popping stops, remove the lid and season with salt to taste, then tip into a bowl. Reheat the honey, pour over the popcorn and serve.

Corn Cobs with Chilli and Thyme

Butter Peel off the husks from 4 fresh corn on the cob, then pull off the silks and cut off the stalks. Cook in a saucepan of salted boiling water for 10–12 minutes. Meanwhile, beat together 2 tablespoons softened butter or smen, the juice of ½ lemon, 1–2 teaspoons finely chopped dried red chilli, 2 teaspoons dried thyme and 1–2 crushed garlic cloves in a bowl, then season well. Drain the corn, then refresh under cold running water and pat dry. Smear the chilli and thyme butter over the corn, then place in a baking tray. Place in a preheated oven, 180°C (350°F), Gas Mark 4, for 15 minutes, turning occasionally until golden brown. Serve hot.

MOR-SOUP-QAC

30 Cheese and Paprika Potato Cakes

Serves 4

700 g (1½ lb) small equal-sized
  potatoes
225 g (7½ oz) hard, tangy sheep's
  or mature Cheddar cheese,
  finely diced
1–2 teaspoon cumin seeds
2 teaspoons smoked paprika
4 tablespoons plain flour
sunflower or vegetable oil,
  for shallow-frying
salt and pepper
lemon wedges, to garnish
dips or chutneys, to serve
  (optional)

- Cook the potatoes in a saucepan of boiling water for 10–12 minutes until soft. Drain, then refresh under cold running water and peel off the skins. Place in a bowl and roughly mash with a fork until still a little chunky. Add the cheese, cumin seeds and paprika and season.

- Tip the flour onto a plate. Divide the potato mixture into 12 pieces, shape each piece into a ball, then flatten slightly and dip into the flour to lightly coat on both sides.

- Heat a thin layer of oil in a large, heavy-based frying pan, add the potato cakes and cook for about 8 minutes, turning occasionally, until crispy and golden brown. Drain on kitchen paper, sprinkle with a little extra sea salt, garnish with lemon wedges and serve with dips or chutneys, if liked.

 Paprika and Herb Cheese

Place 300 g (10 oz) feta cheese, cut into bite-sized pieces, in a shallow serving dish. Drizzle over 2 tablespoons olive oil, dust with 1–2 teaspoons hot paprika and scatter over a finely chopped small bunch of flat leaf parsley. Serve with chunks of crusty bread to mop up the oil.

 Paprika and Herb Cheesy Mashed Potatoes Cook 700 g (1½ lb) potatoes, peeled and roughly chopped, in a saucepan of boiling water for about 10 minutes until soft. Drain, then return to the pan and roughly mash with a fork. Beat in 225 g (7½ oz) coarsely grated hard sheep's, feta or Cheddar cheese while the potatoes are still hot. Add 1–2 teaspoons smoked paprika and a finely chopped small bunch of flat leaf parsley and season. Serve with dollops of creamy yogurt and pickled chillies.

MOR-SOUP-VIY

QuickCook

Couscous, K'dras and Tagines

Recipes listed by cooking time

30

20

10

10 Quick Cinnamon Couscous

Serves 4

350 g (11½ oz) couscous
2 tablespoons butter or ghee
1 teaspoon cinnamon
1 teaspoon icing sugar (optional)
salt and pepper

- Tip the couscous into a heatproof bowl and just cover with boiling water. Cover with clingfilm and leave to stand for 5 minutes, then fluff up with a fork.

- Melt the butter or ghee in a large frying pan, add the couscous, stirring well to separate the grains, and season.

- Spoon the couscous into a pyramid on a serving dish and dust with the cinnamon and icing sugar, if using. Serve hot as a side dish.

 Buttered Almond and Cinnamon Couscous Tip 350 g (11½ oz) couscous into a bowl. Stir ½ teaspoon salt into 400 ml (14 fl oz) warm water, pour over the couscous and mix well. Cover with a clean tea towel and leave to stand for about 10 minutes. Melt 2 tablespoons butter or ghee in a heavy-based frying pan, stir in 2 tablespoons flaked almonds and cook for 2–3 minutes until golden brown. Add the couscous and toss well. Serve hot as a side dish, dusted with a little ground cinnamon.

 Buttery Couscous with Cinnamon Tip 350 g (11½ oz) couscous into an ovenproof dish. Stir ½ teaspoon salt into 400 ml (14 fl oz) warm water and pour over the couscous. Cover with a clean tea towel and leave to stand for about 10 minutes. Using your fingers, rub 2 tablespoons sunflower or olive oil into the grains to break up the lumps. Lift the couscous into the air and let it fall back into the dish so that the grains feel light and airy. Scatter over 25 g (1 oz) butter, cut into small pieces, and cover with a piece of damp greaseproof paper. Place in a preheated oven, 180°C (350°F), Gas Mark 4, for about 15 minutes until heated through. Fluff up with a fork and serve as a side dish, dusted with 1 scant teaspoon cinnamon.

MOR-COUS-TAX

20 Spicy Pine Nut and Apricot Couscous

Serves 4

1–2 tablespoons butter or ghee
1 teaspoon cumin seeds
1 teaspoon coriander seeds
1 teaspoon fennel seeds
2 tablespoons toasted pine nuts
2–3 tablespoons finely chopped
ready-to-eat dried apricots
1–2 teaspoons harissa paste
(see page 70)
salt and pepper

For the couscous

350 g (11½ oz) couscous
½ teaspoon salt
400 ml (14 fl oz) warm water
1–2 tablespoons sunflower oil

- Tip the couscous into a heatproof bowl. Stir the salt into the measurement water and pour over the couscous. Cover with a clean tea towel and leave to stand for about 10 minutes. Using your fingers, rub the oil into the grains for 4–5 minutes until light, airy and any lumps are broken up.

- Heat the butter or ghee in a heavy-based frying pan, stir in the spices and fry for 2 minutes until they emit a nutty aroma. Toss in the pine nuts, apricots and harissa, then add the couscous, mix well and season.

 Quick Spicy Pine Nut Couscous

Tip 350 g (11½ oz) couscous into a heatproof bowl and just cover with boiling water. Cover with clingfilm and leave to stand for 5 minutes, then fluff up with a fork. Heat 1–2 tablespoons ghee in a large, heavy-based frying pan, add 2 teaspoons harissa paste (see page 70) and stir in the couscous, mix well and cook until heated through. Season, then serve scattered with 1 tablespoon toasted pine nuts.

 Spicy Pistachio, Pine Nut and Date Couscous Prepare 350 g (11½ oz) couscous as above. Dry-fry 120 g (4 oz) shelled unsalted pistachio nuts and 2 tablespoons pine nuts in a heavy-based frying pan over a medium heat until they begin to colour and emit a nutty aroma. Melt 1–2 tablespoons ghee in a separate large, heavy-based pan, stir in the toasted pistachios, most of the pine nuts and 1 teaspoon cardamom seeds. Stir in 120 g (4 oz) finely sliced ready-to-eat soft pitted dates, a pinch of saffron threads and 1–2 teaspoons ras el hanout and cook for 1–2 minutes. Add the prepared couscous, mix well and heat through, then season. Turn off the heat, cover with a clean tea towel and leave to steam for 5 minutes. Toss over a high heat, then serve scattered with the reserved pine nuts and sprinkled with 2 teaspoons ground cinnamon. Serve immediately.

30 Couscous Tfaia with Beef

Serves 4

500 g (1 lb) beef, cut into strips
1 onion, finely chopped
1 teaspoon ground coriander
1 teaspoon ground cumin
pinch of saffron threads
1 quantity couscous (see
    30-minute recipe, page 134)

For the tfaia

1 teaspoon saffron threads
2 tablespoons warm water
1 tablespoon olive oil
1 tablespoon butter
2 onions, thinly sliced
2 tablespoons sultanas
2–3 cinnamon sticks
2 tablespoons honey
salt and pepper

- Place the beef in a heavy-based saucepan or the base of a tagine with the onion and spices. Pour in just enough water to cover and bring to the boil. Reduce the heat, cover and simmer for 25–30 minutes.

- Meanwhile, prepare and cook the couscous following the 30-minute method on page 134.

- To make the tfaia, place the saffron in a small bowl, add the measurement water and leave to soak. Heat the oil and butter in a heavy-based frying pan, stir in the onions and cook for 2–3 minutes. Add the sultanas, cinnamon sticks, saffron water and honey and season. Reduce the heat, cover and cook gently for 10–15 minutes.

- Remove the beef from the cooking liquid, spoon over the couscous on a serving plate and top with the tfaia. Strain the liquid into a jug and serve separately.

1 Simple Harissa Beef Couscous

Heat 2 tablespoons ghee in a heavy-based frying pan, stir in 2 finely chopped garlic cloves and 1 tablespoon peeled and finely chopped fresh root ginger and cook for 2–3 minutes. Stir in 225 g (7½ oz) lean beef, very finely sliced, and cook for 2–3 minutes. Meanwhile, tip 350 g (11½ oz) couscous into a heatproof bowl and just cover with boiling water. Cover with clingfilm and leave to stand for 5 minutes, then fluff up with a fork. Add with 1–2 teaspoons harissa paste (see page 70) to the beef, mix well and heat through. Season and serve garnished with some finely chopped coriander.

2 Couscous Tfaia

Heat 2 tablespoons ghee in a frying pan, stir in 3 sliced onions and 1 tablespoon chopped fresh root ginger. Cook for 3–4 minutes. Add 2 tablespoons sultanas, 3–4 cinnamon sticks, 1 teaspoon saffron threads soaked in 2 tablespoons water and 2 tablespoons honey. Cover and cook gently for 10–15 minutes. Season. Meanwhile, prepare 350 g (11½ oz) couscous following the 20-minute method on page 138, omitting the lemon rind and pepper. Serve with the tfaia, garnished with chopped coriander.

MOR-COUS-XUA

30 Couscous with Spring Vegetables and Dill

Serves 4

850 ml (1½ pints) hot vegetable or chicken stock
pinch of saffron threads
175 g (6 oz) fresh broad beans, podded
2–3 fresh or frozen ready-prepared artichoke bottoms, cut into quarters
4 baby courgettes, sliced thickly
4 garlic cloves, finely sliced
150 g (5 oz) fresh peas, podded
4–6 spring onions, thickly sliced
small bunch of dill, finely chopped
salt and pepper

For the couscous

450 g (14½ oz) couscous
½ teaspoon salt
500 ml (17 fl oz) warm water
1–2 tablespoons olive oil
15 g (½ oz) butter, cut into small pieces

- Tip the couscous into an ovenproof dish. Stir the salt into the measurement water and pour over the couscous. Cover with a clean tea towel and leave to stand for about 10 minutes. Using your fingers, rub the oil into the grains until light, airy and any lumps are broken up. Scatter over the butter and cover with a piece of damp greaseproof paper. Place in a preheated oven, 180°C (350°F), Gas Mark 4, for about 10–15 minutes until heated through.

- Meanwhile, bring the stock and saffron to the boil in a heavy-based saucepan. Drop in the broad beans, artichoke bottoms, courgettes and garlic and cook for 2–3 minutes. Add the peas and spring onions, reduce the heat and simmer for 10 minutes until the vegetables are tender. Season and stir in the dill.

- Using a slotted spoon, remove the vegetables from the broth and arrange over the couscous in a shallow serving dish. Drizzle with a little broth and serve the remaining broth separately in a jug.

 Speedy Herb Couscous

Tip 350 g (11½ oz) couscous into a heatproof bowl and just cover with boiling water. Cover with clingfilm and leave to stand for 5 minutes, then fluff with a fork. Stir in 2 tablespoons olive oil to separate the grains, then toss in the juice of 1 lemon and 1 tablespoon each of finely chopped flat leaf parsley, coriander and mint. Season and serve as a side dish.

 Preserved Lemon and Herb Couscous

Salad Tip 350 g (11½ oz) couscous into a bowl. Stir ½ teaspoon salt into 400 ml (14 fl oz) warm water and pour over the couscous. Cover with a clean tea towel and leave to stand for about 10 minutes. Using your fingertips, rub 1–2 tablespoons olive oil into the grains for 4–5 minutes until light, airy and any lumps are broken up. Add 2–3 finely chopped spring onions, 1 deseeded and finely chopped green chilli, the finely chopped rind of 1 preserved lemon (see page 68) and 2 tablespoons each of finely chopped flat leaf parsley, mint and coriander. Season, toss well and serve.

MOR-COUS-DAA

30 Couscous with Orangey Fennel and Courgette

Serves 4

2 tablespoons olive oil
1–2 teaspoons aniseed seeds
grated rind of 1 orange
2 fennel bulbs, trimmed and cut
    into quarters
juice of 2 oranges
1 courgette, halved and sliced
    lengthways
15 g (½ oz) butter
1 tablespoon runny honey
1 tablespoon orange blossom water
salt and pepper
½ orange, thinly sliced, to garnish

For the couscous

350 g (11½ oz) couscous
½ teaspoon salt
400 ml (14 fl oz) warm water
2 tablespoons olive oil
15 g (½ oz) butter, in small pieces

- Prepare and cook the couscous following the 30-minute method on page 134.

- Meanwhile, heat the oil in a heavy-based frying pan or the base of a tagine, stir in the aniseed and orange rind and cook for 1–2 minutes until fragrant. Toss in the fennel and coat well, then pour in the orange juice. Cover and cook gently for 3–4 minutes.

- Add the courgette and butter, season and drizzle over the honey. Cover and cook for a further 3–4 minutes until the vegetables are very tender. Remove the lid and bubble up any liquid for 3–4 minutes until slightly caramelized, then pour over the orange blossom water.

- Spoon the fennel and courgette over the couscous in a shallow serving dish. Drizzle over the caramelized juice and garnish with the orange slices.

 Fennel and Onion Couscous

Tip 350 g (11½ oz) couscous into a heatproof bowl and just cover with boiling water. Cover with clingfilm and leave to stand for 5 minutes. Meanwhile, heat 1 tablespoon each of olive oil and butter in a frying pan, stir in 1–2 teaspoons fennel seeds, 1 sliced red onion and 1 trimmed and sliced fennel bulb and cook for 4–5 minutes. Season and toss in the couscous. Serve as a side dish with lemon wedges.

 Fennel, Orange and Zahtar

Couscous Prepare and heat 350 g (11½ oz) couscous following the 20-minute method on page 138, omitting the lemon rind and pepper. Meanwhile, put 2 trimmed and finely sliced fennel bulbs into a grill pan. Drizzle with 2 tablespoons olive oil, season and cook under a preheated hot grill for 10 minutes until tender and beginning to colour. Remove the peel and pith from 1 orange, then thinly slice and quarter the slices, removing any seeds. Scatter over the fennel. Drizzle with 1–2 teaspoons runny honey and grill for a further 2–3 minutes. Spoon over the couscous on a serving dish. Melt ½ tablespoon butter in the grill pan and drizzle over. Sprinkle over 1–2 teaspoons zahtar and serve hot.

Lemon Couscous with Spicy Shellfish

Serves 6–8

2–3 tablespoons olive oil

750 g (1½ lb) shop-bought ready-prepared seafood selection

2 teaspoons harissa paste (see page 70)

bunch of coriander, finely chopped

salt and pepper

For the lemon couscous

450 g (14½ oz) couscous

2 tablespoons sunflower oil

finely chopped rind of 1 preserved lemon (see page 68)

25 g (1 oz) butter, in small pieces

- Tip the couscous into a heatproof bowl and just cover with boiling water. Cover with clingfilm and leave to stand for 5 minutes. Fluff up with a fork, then stir in the oil to separate the grains. Tip into an ovenproof dish, stir in the preserved lemon rind, season with pepper and scatter over the butter. Cover with a damp piece of greaseproof paper and place in a preheated oven, 180°C (350°F), Gas Mark 4, for 10 minutes until heated through.

- Meanwhile, heat the olive oil in a heavy-based frying pan, add the seafood and cook for 3–4 minutes. Add the harissa, season and stir in most of the coriander.

- Spoon the seafood over the couscous in a shallow serving dish and serve garnished with the remaining coriander.

 Lemon Couscous with Steamed Shellfish Cook 400 g (13 oz) lemon couscous according to the packet instructions. Meanwhile, steam 750 g (1½ lb) raw peeled prawns or scallops for 3–4 minutes until opaque, then tip into a bowl and add 2–3 tablespoons olive oil, the grated rind and juice of 2 limes, 2 crushed garlic cloves, 2 deseeded and finely sliced green chillies and a finely chopped small bunch of mint. Season, toss well and serve with the couscous.

 Lemon Couscous with Shellfish K'dra Heat 2 tablespoons olive or argan oil in a large copper or heavy-based saucepan, stir in 2 teaspoons each of cumin seeds and coriander seeds, 2–3 teaspoons deseeded and finely chopped red chillies and 1–2 teaspoons sugar and cook for 1–2 minutes until fragrant. Stir in 2 teaspoons turmeric, a 400 g (13 oz) can tomatoes, drained of juice, 150 ml (¼ pint) white wine, 850 ml (1½ pints) hot fish stock, 4 finely sliced garlic cloves, 50 g (2 oz) fresh root ginger, peeled and finely sliced, and a finely chopped small bunch each of flat leaf parsley and coriander and bring to the boil, then reduce the heat and simmer for 15 minutes. Season and bring to the boil, then add 250 g (8 oz) raw peeled prawns, 250 g (8 oz) live mussels, cleaned following the instructions on page 86, and 250 g (8 oz) scallops, cover and cook for 5–8 minutes until the mussels open and the prawns and scallops are opaque. Discard any mussels that remain shut. Meanwhile, prepare the Lemon Couscous as above, then serve with the shellfish and stock, garnished with extra chopped herbs.

MOR-COUS-PAU

30 Ginger and Honey Lamb and Apricot Tagine

Serves 4

1–2 tablespoons olive or argan oil

1 onion, finely chopped

2–3 garlic cloves, finely chopped

25 g (1 oz) fresh root ginger, peeled and finely chopped

450 g (14½ oz) lean lamb, cut into bite-sized pieces

2 teaspoons ground cinnamon

175 g (6 oz) ready-to-eat dried apricots

2 large tablespoons runny honey

salt and pepper

Buttery Couscous (see page 128), to serve

- Heat the oil in a large, heavy-based saucepan or the base of a tagine, stir in the onion, garlic and ginger and cook for 1–2 minutes. Add the lamb and toss to coat well, then add the cinnamon. Pour in enough hot water to just cover the meat and bring to the boil. Reduce the heat, cover and simmer for 15 minutes.

- Add the apricots and honey, re-cover and simmer for a further 10 minutes. Season to taste and serve hot with the couscous.

 Quick Ginger and Honey Lamb
Heat 1–2 tablespoons ghee in a large, heavy-based saucepan or the base of a tagine, stir in 2 finely chopped garlic cloves, 2 teaspoons cumin seeds and 25 g (1 oz) fresh root ginger, peeled and finely chopped, and cook for 2 minutes. Add 500 g (1 lb) cubed lamb and cook for a further 5–6 minutes until browned and cooked through. Stir in 1 tablespoon runny honey, season and toss in 1 tablespoon finely chopped coriander. Serve with couscous.

 Spicy Ginger and Honey Lamb
Tagine Heat 1–2 tablespoons olive oil in a large, heavy-based saucepan or the base of a tagine, stir in 1 chopped onion, 2 chopped garlic cloves, 1–2 deseeded and finely chopped red chillies and 25 g (1 oz) fresh root ginger, peeled and chopped, and cook for 1–2 minutes. Stir in 500 g (1 lb) cubed lamb, 2 tablespoons runny honey and enough hot water to cover. Bring to the boil, cover and simmer for 15 minutes. Season to taste and toss in 1 tablespoon finely chopped coriander. Serve with plain buttery couscous or a herb couscous.

10 Spicy Beef, Sun-Dried Tomatoes and Pine Nuts

Serves 4

2 tablespoons pine nuts

250 g (8 oz) ready-cooked lean beef, cut into thin strips

150 g (5 oz) sun-dried tomatoes in oil, drained and cut into strips

2–3 tablespoons olive or argan oil

juice of 1 lemon

1 teaspoon harissa paste (see page 70)

bunch of flat leaf parsley, chopped

salt and pepper

couscous, to serve (optional)

- Dry-fry the pine nuts in a small, heavy-based frying pan over a medium heat for 2 minutes until golden brown.

- Put the beef, tomatoes and most of the toasted pine nuts in a bowl. Mix together the oil, lemon juice, harissa and parsley in a separate bowl and season. Pour over the beef and toss well.

- Scatter with the reserved pine nuts and serve with couscous, if liked.

 Turmeric Beef and Sun-Dried Tomato Tagine Heat 2 tablespoons ghee in a large saucepan or the base of a tagine, stir in 2 chopped garlic cloves, 2 deseeded and chopped red chillies, 1 tablespoon chopped root ginger and 1 teaspoon sugar and cook for 2–3 minutes. Add 450 g (14½ oz) beef, cut into strips and tossed in 1 tablespoon turmeric, coat well and cook for 1–2 minutes, then add 120 g (4 oz) sun-dried tomatoes in oil, drained and sliced, and 1 tablespoon chopped coriander. Pour in enough water to just cover the base of the pan, drizzle with 2 teaspoons honey, cover and cook for 15 minutes. Season, garnish with a little more finely chopped coriander and serve with chunks of crusty bread or couscous.

 Beef, Aubergine and Sun-Dried Tomato Tagine Cut 1 aubergine into bite-sized pieces, place in a colander and sprinkle with salt. Meanwhile, heat 2–3 tablespoons argan oil or ghee in a large, heavy-based saucepan or the base of a tagine, stir in 2 finely chopped onions, 4 finely chopped garlic cloves, 1–2 deseeded and finely chopped red chillies, 25 g (1 oz) fresh root ginger, peeled and finely chopped, and 2 teaspoons coriander seeds and cook for 2–3 minutes. Add 1 tablespoon crumbled dried sage leaves and 450 g (14½ oz) lean beef, cut into bite-sized pieces, and stir well to coat. Pour in 500 ml (17 fl oz) hot beef or chicken stock, bring to the boil, then reduce the heat, cover and simmer for 10 minutes. Rinse the aubergines and pat dry, then stir into the beef, re-cover and cook for a further 10 minutes. Add 125 g (4 oz) sun-dried tomatoes in oil, drained and roughly chopped, and 1 tablespoon runny honey. Season, re-cover and continue to cook for 5 minutes. Scatter over a finely chopped bunch of flat leaf parsley and serve with chunks of crusty bread or couscous.

30 Chicken, Green Olive and Preserved Lemon Tagine

Serves 4

1–2 tablespoons olive or argan oil
2 garlic cloves, finely chopped
1 onion, finely chopped
1 teaspoon coriander seeds
1 teaspoon cumin seeds
8 chicken thighs
juice of 1 lemon
pinch of saffron threads
2 cinnamon sticks
25 g (1 oz) butter
rind of 1 preserved lemon, cut
   into thin strips (see page 68)
175 g (6 oz) cracked green olives
salt and pepper
Buttery Couscous (see page 128),
   to serve (optional)

- Heat the oil in a large, heavy-based saucepan or the base of a tagine, stir in the garlic, onion and coriander and cumin seeds and cook for 1–2 minutes. Add the chicken thighs and lightly brown on each side.

- Pour in the lemon juice and enough water to just cover the chicken. Stir in the saffron, cinnamon sticks and butter and bring to the boil, then reduce the heat, cover and simmer for 15 minutes.

- Add the preserved lemon rind and olives, re-cover and simmer for a further 10 minutes. Season to taste and serve hot with the couscous, if liked.

 Spicy Chicken and Preserved Lemon Pittas Heat 2 tablespoons olive oil and a knob of butter in a frying pan or tagine, stir in 2 crushed garlic cloves and cook for 1 minute, then stir in 1–2 teaspoons harissa paste (see page 70) and 250–350 g (8–11½ oz) ready-cooked chicken, cut into strips and tossed with 2 teaspoons turmeric. Heat through, then add 1 tablespoon chopped preserved lemon rind (see page 68) and 1 tablespoon chopped coriander. Season and spoon into 4 pitta breads. Serve with dollops of natural yogurt and a sprinkling of chopped flat leaf parsley.

 Spicy Chicken and Preserved Lemon Tagine Heat 1–2 tablespoons olive oil in a large, heavy-based saucepan or the base of a tagine, stir in 2 finely chopped garlic cloves, 1 finely chopped onion, 1 deseeded and finely chopped red chilli and 2 teaspoons coriander seeds and cook for 1–2 minutes. Toss in 450 g (14½ oz) diced or sliced skinless chicken breast fillet and cook for 2–3 minutes until browned, then pour in 125 ml (4 fl oz) white wine and enough water to just cover the chicken and bring to the boil. Reduce the heat, cover and simmer for 10 minutes. Add the finely chopped rind of 1 preserved lemon (see page 68), re-cover and simmer for a further 5 minutes until the chicken is cooked through. Season to taste and serve scattered with 1 tablespoon finely chopped flat leaf parsley. Serve with a herb couscous.

Chermoula Monkfish and Black Olive Tagine

Serves 4

700 g (1¼ lb) monkfish tail,
  cut into bite-sized pieces
2 tablespoons ready-made
  chermoula paste
2 tablesoons olive oil
2 tablespoons marinated black
  olives, drained and pitted
50 ml (2 fl oz) fino sherry
salt and pepper

To garnish
smoked paprika
finely chopped flat leaf parsley

- Place the monkfish tail in a bowl, rub with the chermoula and leave to marinate for 5 minutes.

- Heat the oil in a heavy-based frying pan or the base of a tagine, stir in the monkfish, olives and sherry, cover and cook for 10–15 minutes until the fish is cooked through. Season, then serve sprinkled with a little paprika and parsley.

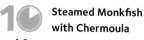

Steamed Monkfish with Chermoula and Couscous Line a steamer with coriander leaves and place 700 g (1¼ lb) monkfish tail, cut into bite-sized pieces, on top. Steam for 8–10 minutes until just cooked through and tender. Season and serve hot with a bowl of ready-made chermoula paste for dipping. Serve with a herb or spicy couscous.

Monkfish, Potato and Chermoula Tagine Using a pestle and mortar, pound 1 garlic clove and 1 teaspoon sea salt to a smooth paste. Stir in 2 teaspoons ground cumin, 1–2 teaspoons smoked paprika, the juice of 1 lemon and a roughly chopped small bunch of coriander, then mix with 2 tablespoons olive oil. Reserve 1 tablespoon, then rub the rest over 700 g (1¼ lb) monkfish and leave to marinate for at least 10 minutes to let the flavours mingle. Meanwhile, par-boil 8 peeled new potatoes in a saucepan of boiling water for 6–8 minutes, or until slightly softened. Drain, refresh under cold running water and cut in half lengthways. Heat 1 tablespoon olive oil in a frying pan or the base of a tagine, stir in 1 crushed garlic clove and cook until it begins to colour, then add the potatoes and the reserved chermoula and season. Top with the marinated fish, scatter over 10–12 cherry tomatoes and drizzle with 1 tablespoon olive oil. Pour in 100 ml (3½ fl oz) water, cover and cook over a medium heat for 10–15 minutes until cooked through. Season and gently stir together. Serve immediately with warm crusty bread to mop up the juices.

MOR-COUS-KUT

30 Lamb, Sweet Potato and Okra K'dra

Serves 6–8

2 tablespoons smen or ghee

3 onions, finely sliced

2–3 teaspoons coriander seeds

2–3 cinnamon sticks

1 teaspoon black peppercorns

pinch of saffron threads

500 g (1 lb) lean lamb, cut into
bite-sized pieces

1.2 litres (2 pints) hot lamb or
chicken stock

2 sweet potatoes, peeled and
cut into bite-sized pieces

1 tablespoon butter

250 g (8 oz) fresh okra

juice of 1 lemon

salt

couscous, to serve (optional)

- Heat the smen or ghee in a large copper or heavy-based saucepan, stir in the onions and cook for 1–2 minutes. Add the coriander seeds, cinnamon sticks, peppercorns, saffron and lamb and mix well.

- Pour in the stock and bring to the boil, then cover, reduce the heat and cook gently for 10 minutes. Add the sweet potatoes and butter, re-cover and cook gently for a further 10 minutes.

- Meanwhile, place the okra in a non-metallic bowl, pour over the lemon juice and leave to stand for 10 minutes, then drain.

- Add the okra to the pan and simmer for a further 5–8 minutes until cooked through but still retaining a crunch. Season with salt. Serve the lamb and vegetables with couscous, if liked, pouring the sauce into a bowl to serve separately.

1 Buttered Okra with Preserved Lemon

Place 450 g (14½ oz) okra in a non-metallic bowl, pour over the juice of 2 lemons and leave to stand for 3–4 minutes, then drain well. Heat 2 tablespoons olive oil in a heavy-based frying pan or the base of a tagine, add the okra and cook for 4–5 minutes. Stir in the sliced rind of 1 preserved lemon (see page 68) and season. Pour over 1 tablespoon melted butter and serve with plain buttery couscous.

2 Quick Lamb, Lemon and Okra

K'dra Heat 2 tablespoons smen or ghee in a large copper or heavy-based saucepan, stir in 3 finely sliced onions, 2 teaspoons coriander seeds, 2 cinnamon sticks and a pinch of saffron threads and cook for 2–3 minutes. Add 450 g (14½ oz) lean lamb, cut into thin strips, mix well and add 1 lemon, cut into 6 segments. Pour in 850 ml (1½ pints) hot lamb or chicken stock, cover and cook over a medium heat for 12–15 minutes until cooked through. Meanwhile, place 225 g (7½ oz) fresh okra in a non-metallic bowl, pour over the juice of 1 lemon and leave to stand for 5 minutes, then drain. Add to the lamb 5 minutes before the end of the cooking time. Season and stir in a roughly chopped small bunch of flat leaf parsley. Serve with couscous, pouring the sauce into a bowl to serve with it.

30 Beef, Prune and Almond Tagine

Serves 4

1–2 tablespoons ghee

1 onion, finely chopped

2–3 garlic cloves, finely chopped

25 g (1 oz) fresh root ginger, peeled and finely chopped

450 g (14½ oz) lean beef, cut into bite-sized pieces

1–2 teaspoons ras el hanout

175 g (6 oz) ready-to-eat pitted dried prunes

125 g (4 oz) blanched almonds

2 tablespoons runny honey

salt and pepper

finely chopped flat leaf parsley, to garnish

Buttery Couscous (see page 128), to serve

- Heat the ghee in a large, heavy-based saucepan or the base of a tagine, stir in the onion, garlic and ginger and cook for 1–2 minutes. Add the beef and coat well, then add the ras el hanout.

- Pour in enough water to just cover the meat and bring to the boil. Reduce the heat, cover and simmer for 15 minutes.

- Add the prunes and almonds and stir in the honey. Season, bring back to the boil, re-cover and cook over a medium heat for a further 10 minutes. Garnish with parsley and serve with couscous.

 Almond-Stuffed Prunes in Orange Syrup Open up 12 ready-to-eat pitted dried prunes and stuff each one with a blanched almond. Place the prunes in a frying pan or the base of a tagine, pour over the juice of 2 oranges and 2 tablespoons orange blossom water and drizzle over 1 tablespoon honey. Bring to the boil, cover and cook over a medium heat for 8–9 minutes. Baste the prunes in the syrupy juice, dust with 1 teaspoon ground cinnamon and serve with tagines and couscous.

 Almond and Ginger Beef Tagine Heat 1–2 tablespoons ghee in a large, heavy-based saucepan or the base of a tagine, stir in 2 finely chopped garlic cloves, 2 teaspoons coriander seeds, 1 teaspoon finely chopped dried red chilli and 50 g (2 oz) fresh root ginger, peeled and finely chopped, and cook for 1–2 minutes. Add 500 g (1 lb) lean beef, cut into thin strips, mix well and cook for 2–3 minutes. Add 120 g (4 oz) sliced blanched almonds, 1 tablespoon honey and 400 ml (14 fl oz) water and bring to the boil, then cover and cook over a medium heat for 15 minutes. Season, garnish with a finely chopped small bunch of coriander and serve with couscous.

30 Meatball and Egg Tagine with Toasted Cumin

Serves 4

600 ml (1 pint) water
1 tablespoon butter
1 teaspoon salt
½ teaspoon cayenne powder
4 eggs
1–2 teaspoons cumin seeds
small bunch of flat leaf parsley,
  finely chopped, to garnish
buttered toasted flatbreads,
  to serve (optional)

For the meatballs

225 g (7½ oz) lean minced lamb
1 onion, finely chopped
1–2 teaspoons dried mint
1–2 teaspoons ground cinnamon
1–2 teaspoons ras el hanout
salt and pepper

- To make the meatballs, mix together all the ingredients in a bowl and season. Knead the mixture well, then roll cherry-sized pieces into firm balls. Pour the measurement water into a large saucepan or the base of a tagine and bring to the boil. Add the meatballs, a few at a time, and poach for about 10 minutes, turning occasionally, until cooked through. Remove with a slotted spoon and drain on kitchen paper.

- Pour about 125 ml (4 fl oz) of the cooking liquid into a saucepan or the base of a tagine and bring to the boil. Stir in the butter, salt and cayenne, then add the meatballs. Make 4 wells, then break the eggs into the wells, cover and cook for 5–6 minutes until the whites are just set but the yolks are still runny.

- Meanwhile, dry-fry the cumin seeds in a small, heavy-based frying pan over a medium heat for 1–2 minutes until they emit a nutty aroma. Tip into a spice grinder and grind over the eggs. Garnish with the parsley and serve immediately, with buttered toasted flatbreads, if liked.

---

10 Eggs with Toasted Cumin

Heat 1 tablespoon ghee in a large, heavy-based frying pan or the base of a tagine, break in 6–8 eggs and sprinkle over a little paprika and salt. Cover and cook gently until the whites are firm. Meanwhile, dry-fry 1–2 teaspoons cumin seeds as above. Place in a spice grinder and grind over the eggs. Serve with buttered toasted flatbreads.

20 Meatball, Toasted Cumin and Egg

Tagine Mix together 250 g (8 oz) lean minced lamb, 1 very finely chopped onion, 1 tablespoon very finely chopped parsley and 1–2 teaspoons ras el hanout in a bowl and season. Knead and shape the mixture as above. Heat 1–2 tablespoons ghee in a heavy-based frying pan or the base of a tagine, stir in 2 teaspoons cumin seeds, toasted as above, and cook for 1 minute. Add the meatballs and cook for 2–3 minutes, then pour in 300 ml (½ pint) water and season. Bring to the boil, cover and cook over a medium heat for 10–12 minutes until cooked through. Meanwhile, soft-boil 2 eggs, then drain, shell and roughly chop. Scatter over the meatballs, garnish with a finely chopped small bunch of coriander and serve with couscous.

Toasted Saffron, Herb and Preserved Lemon Fish Tagine

Serves 4

pinch of saffron threads

300 ml (½ pint) warm water

1–2 tablespoons olive oil

finely sliced rind of 1 preserved lemon (see page 68)

500 g (1 lb) skinless firm fish fillets, such as sea bass, cut into chunks

small bunch of mint, finely chopped

salt and pepper

couscous, to serve (optional)

- Dry-fry the saffron in a small frying pan over a medium heat for less than a minute until it emits a faint aroma. Using a pestle and mortar or spice grinder, grind to a powder, then stir in the measurement water until the saffron dissolves.

- Heat the oil in a heavy-based saucepan or the base of a tagine, stir in the preserved lemon rind, fish, most of the mint and the saffron water and bring to the boil. Season, cover and cook gently, stirring occasionally, for 15 minutes until the fish is cooked through. Garnish with the reserved mint and serve with couscous, if liked.

10 Sea Bass with Olives, Saffron and Preserved Lemon

Heat 2 tablespoons olive oil in a heavy-based saucepan or the base of a tagine, stir in a pinch of saffron threads, 2 tablespoons finely sliced green olives and 1 tablespoon finely sliced preserved lemon rind (see page 68) and cook for 1–2 minutes. Add 500 g (1 lb) skinless firm fish fillets, such as sea bass, cut into bite-sized pieces, and cook for a further 2–3 minutes. Season, cover and cook over a low heat for 5 minutes until the fish is just cooked through. Serve with couscous.

30 Toasted Saffron, Preserved Lemon, Potato and Fish Tagine

Par-boil 500 g (1 lb) new potatoes in a saucepan of boiling water for about 8 minutes, or until slightly softened. Meanwhile, dry-fry and grind a pinch of saffron threads as above, then stir in 150 ml (¼ pint) warm water until the saffron dissolves. Set aside. Cut 4 tomatoes into slices. Drain the potatoes, then refresh under cold running water and peel off the skins. Cut into thick slices. Heat 2 tablespoons olive oil in a large, heavy-based saucepan or the base of a tagine, stir in 4–6 peeled and smashed garlic cloves and cook for 1–2 minutes until beginning to colour. Reduce the heat to low and line the pan with the potatoes, followed by a layer of the tomatoes, reserving a few slices. Scatter over the finely sliced rind of ½ preserved lemon (see page 68) and ½ finely chopped small bunch of flat leaf parsley and top with 500 g (1 lb) sea bass fillets, skinned and cut into chunks. Mix together the saffron water, the juice of 1 lemon and 1 tablespoon olive oil and season well. Pour over the fish, top with the reserved tomatoes and sprinkle with another layer of preserved lemon rind and parsley. Cover and cook over a medium heat for 15 minutes until the fish is just cooked through. Serve immediately with couscous.

30 Herby Prawn, Tomato and Turmeric Fennel Tagine

Serves 4

2 fennel bulbs, trimmed and
   thickly sliced lengthways
3 tablespoons olive oil
1 tablespoon butter
2–3 teaspoons turmeric
1 onion, finely chopped
2 garlic cloves, finely chopped
25 g (1 oz) fresh root ginger,
   peeled and finely chopped
500 g (1 lb) raw peeled prawns
1 teaspoon smoked paprika
1 teaspoon sugar
400 g (13 oz) can tomatoes,
   drained of juice
small bunch of coriander, chopped
bunch of flat leaf parsley, chopped
salt and pepper
chunks of crusty bread or
   couscous, to serve (optional)

- Place the fennel in a steamer basket and steam for 5–6 minutes to soften. Refresh under cold running water, drain and pat dry. Heat 1 tablespoon of the oil and the butter in a heavy-based frying pan, add the fennel and cook for 3–4 minutes on each side until golden brown. Toss in 1–2 teaspoons of the turmeric and set aside.

- Heat the remaining oil in a large, heavy-based frying pan or the base of a tagine, stir in the onion, garlic and ginger and cook for 1–2 minutes until beginning to colour. Add the prawns and cook for 2–3 minutes until they turn pink, then stir in the remaining turmeric and the paprika. Add the sugar, tomatoes and half the herbs. Cover and cook gently for 10 minutes.

- Gently stir in the fennel, re-cover and cook for a further 5 minutes. Season, garnish with the remaining herbs and serve with crusty bread or couscous, if liked.

 Spicy Turmeric and Lime Prawns Heat 2 tablespoons olive oil in a frying pan or tagine, stir in 2 chopped garlic cloves, 1–2 deseeded and chopped chillies and 1 tablespoon chopped preserved lemon rind (see page 68) and cook for 1–2 minutes. Stir in 450 g (14½ oz) raw peeled prawns and cook for 2–3 minutes. Stir in 2 teaspoons turmeric and the juice of 2 limes, heat and season. Garnish with a chopped bunch of coriander and serve with warm flatbreads or couscous.

 Turmeric Prawn, Fennel and Tomato Tagine Heat 2–3 tablespoons olive oil in a heavy-based saucepan or the base of a tagine, add 500 g (1 lb) raw peeled prawns and cook for 2–3 minutes until they turn pink. Off the heat, toss in 1–2 teaspoons turmeric, then drain on kitchen paper. Stir 2 finely chopped garlic cloves and 25 g (1 oz) fresh root ginger, peeled and finely chopped, into the pan and cook for 1–2 minutes, then add 2 finely sliced fennel bulbs and cook for a further 2 minutes to soften. Add 1 teaspoon sugar, a 400 g (13 oz) can tomatoes, drained of juice, and 100 ml (3½ fl oz) white wine. Cover and cook over a medium heat for 10 minutes. Season and stir in the prawns. Garnish with 1 tablespoon finely chopped coriander and serve with chunks of crusty bread or couscous.

30 Cinnamon Duck and Caramelized Pear Tagine

Serves 4

2 tablespoons olive oil
2 onions, finely chopped
25 g (1 oz) fresh root ginger,
  peeled and finely chopped
2 cinnamon sticks
pinch of saffron threads
500 g (1 lb) duck breasts, cubed
400 ml (14 fl oz) hot chicken stock
2 tablespoons butter
3–4 tablespoons honey
2 pears, peeled, quartered, cored
2–3 tablespoons orange
  blossom water
salt and pepper
a few shredded lemon balm or
  mint leaves, to garnish
Buttery Couscous (see page 128),
  to serve

- Heat the oil in a heavy-based frying pan or the base of a tagine, stir in the onions and ginger and cook until they begin to colour, then add the cinnamon sticks and saffron. Add the duck meat and coat well. Pour in the stock and bring to the boil. Reduce the heat, cover and cook over a medium heat for 20 minutes.

- Meanwhile, melt the butter in a heavy-based frying pan and stir in the honey. Toss in the pears and cook until they begin to caramelize.

- Add the pears to the duck with the orange blossom water and cook for a further 5 minutes. Season, garnish with the lemon balm or mint and serve with couscous.

 Spiced Duck and Prunes with Cinnamon Heat 2 tablespoons butter in a frying pan or tagine, stir in 1–2 teaspoons coriander seeds, 1 tablespoon chopped fresh root ginger and 175 g (6 oz) sliced pitted prunes and cook for 2 minutes. Add 350 g (11½ oz) shop-bought ready-cooked duck meat, cut into strips, 1 tablespoon honey and 2–3 tablespoons orange blossom water, cover and cook over a medium heat for 6–8 minutes until heated through. Season, dust with cinnamon and serve with couscous.

 Duck, Plum and Cinnamon Tagine Place 6–8 halved and stoned ripe red or purple plums in a blender and whizz to a purée. Heat 2 tablespoons olive oil and a knob of butter in a heavy-based frying pan or the base of a tagine, stir in 2–3 cinnamon sticks, 6 cloves and 1 teaspoon each of cumin seeds and cardamom seeds. Add 450 g (14½ oz) sliced duck breasts and cook for 2–3 minutes, stirring to coat well, then add 1 tablespoon honey and the puréed plums. Cover and cook over a medium heat for 12–15 minutes until cooked through. Season, garnish with a dusting of icing sugar, followed by a dusting of ground cinnamon, and serve with couscous.

10 Cardamom Lamb and Dates

Serves 4

2 tablespoons ghee

2 red chillies, deseeded and
finely sliced

2 garlic cloves, finely chopped

2 teaspoons cardamom seeds

350 g (11½ oz) shop-bought
ready-cooked lamb, cubed

2–3 tablespoons roughly chopped
ready-to-eat dried dates

1 tablespoon runny honey

juice of 1 lemon

salt and pepper

finely chopped rind of ½ preserved
lemon (see page 68), to garnish

flatbreads or couscous, to serve
(optional)

- Heat the ghee in a heavy-based frying pan or the base of
a tagine, stir in the chillies, garlic and cardamom seeds and
cook for 1–2 minutes until they begin to colour. Add the lamb
and cook for 2 minutes.

- Add the dates, honey and lemon juice and season. Cover
and cook gently for 5–6 minutes until heated through.
Garnish with the preserved lemon rind and serve with
flatbreads or couscous, if liked.

---

20 Date, Cardamom and Caramelized Shallot Tagine

Heat 1–2 tablespoons ghee in a frying pan or the base of a tagine, stir in 2 teaspoons cardamom seeds and 2–3 cinnamon sticks and cook for 1 minute. Toss in 12–16 peeled shallots and cook, stirring, for 2–3 minutes until they begin to colour. Stir in 2 tablespoons honey, 225 g (7½ oz) pitted dates and the juice of 1 lemon and season. Cover and cook gently for 15 minutes until the shallots are caramelized. Garnish with the sliced rind of ½ preserved lemon (see page 68) and serve as a side dish.

30 Date, Shallot and Cardamom Lamb

Tagine Heat 2 tablespoons ghee in a heavy-based saucepan or the base of a tagine, add 500 g (1 lb) lean lamb, cut into bite-sized pieces, and cook for 1–2 minutes until browned. Remove the lamb with a slotted spoon and set aside. Stir in 12 shallots and 4 halved garlic cloves and cook for 2–3 minutes until they begin to colour. Add 2 teaspoons turmeric, 8 cardamom pods and 2 cinnamon sticks and the lamb. Pour in enough water or meat stock to just cover and bring to the boil. Cover, reduce the heat and cook gently for 15 minutes. Stir in 1–2 tablespoons runny honey, season and add 225 g (7½ oz) ready-to-eat soft pitted dates, re-cover and cook over a medium heat for 10 minutes. Garnish with the finely sliced rind of ½ preserved lemon (see page 68) and serve with chunks of crusty bread or couscous.

MOR-COUS-VEH

30 Chorizo, Lentil and Fenugreek Tagine

Serves 4

2 tablespoons argan oil or ghee
2 onions, roughly chopped
4 garlic cloves, roughly chopped
500 g (1 lb) chorizo sausage,
   thickly sliced
2 teaspoons turmeric
2 teaspoons ground fenugreek
225 g (7½ oz) brown lentils,
   rinsed, picked over and drained
400 g (13 oz) can chopped
   tomatoes
2 teaspoons sugar
small bunch of coriander, chopped
salt and pepper

To serve

toasted flatbreads
natural yogurt

- Heat the oil in a heavy-based saucepan or the base of a tagine, stir in the onions and garlic and cook for 1–2 minutes until they begin to colour. Toss in the chorizo and cook for 1–2 minutes to flavour the oil. Add the turmeric, fenugreek and lentils and stir to coat well.

- Add the tomatoes and sugar and pour in enough water to cover the lentils by 2.5 cm (1 inch). Bring to the boil, then cover, reduce the heat and cook gently for about 25 minutes until the lentils are tender but not mushy, adding more water if necessary.

- Stir in most of the coriander and season. Garnish with the remaining coriander and serve with toasted flatbreads and dollops of yogurt.

---

1 Chorizo and Raisins with Fenugreek

Heat 1–2 tablespoons ghee in a saucepan or tagine, stir in 2 teaspoons coriander seeds, 2 sliced onions and 1 teaspoon sugar and cook for 2–3 minutes. Toss in 2 tablespoons raisins, 500 g (1 lb) sliced chorizo and 1 teaspoon ground fenugreek. Cover and cook over a medium heat for 4–5 minutes. Season and stir in the chopped rind of ½ preserved lemon (see page 68). Garnish with a chopped bunch of flat leaf parsley and serve with toasted flatbreads and dollops of yogurt.

2 Chorizo, Potato and Fenugreek

Tagine Heat 2 tablespoons argan oil or ghee in a heavy-based saucepan or the base of a tagine, stir in 2–3 crushed garlic cloves and 2 teaspoons coriander seeds and cook for 1 minute. Add 250 g (8 oz) thickly sliced chorizo sausages and cook for 1–2 minutes to flavour the oil. Stir in 1 teaspoon turmeric, 2 teaspoons ground fenugreek and 12 small peeled potatoes and coat well in the oil. Drizzle in 1 tablespoon runny honey and pour in enough water to just cover the potatoes. Bring to the boil, then season, cover and cook over a medium heat for 15 minutes until the potatoes are tender. Garnish with roughly chopped coriander and serve with a salad or couscous.

MOR-COUS-KOC

30 Herby Carrot, Potato and Pea Tagine

Serves 4

2–3 tablespoons olive or argan oil

2 onions, sliced

4 garlic cloves, chopped

25 g (1 oz) fresh root ginger, peeled and chopped

1–2 red chillies, deseeded and chopped

1 teaspoon cumin seeds

1–2 teaspoons turmeric

1 teaspoon paprika

8 small potatoes, peeled

3–4 carrots, peeled and each cut into 3–4 chunks

600 ml (1 pint) hot vegetable or chicken stock

225 g (7½ oz) fresh or frozen garden peas

small bunch of flat leaf parsley, finely chopped

small bunch of mint, finely chopped

3–4 tomatoes, sliced

20 g (¾ oz) butter, cubed

salt and pepper

couscous, to serve (optional)

• Heat the oil in a heavy-based saucepan or the base of a tagine, stir in the onions, garlic, ginger, chillies and cumin seeds and cook for 2–3 minutes. Add the turmeric and paprika and toss in the potatoes and carrots.

• Pour in the stock and bring to the boil. Cover, reduce the heat and cook gently for 15 minutes until the vegetables are tender.

• Stir in the peas and half the herbs. Season and top with the tomato slices. Scatter over the butter and sprinkle with the remaining herbs. Re-cover and cook for a further 5–10 minutes. Serve with couscous, if liked.

---

10 Preserved Lemon and Sage Carrots

Heat 1 tablespoon olive oil and 25 g (1 oz) butter in a frying pan or tagine, stir in 2–3 peeled and sliced carrots, the sliced rind of 1 preserved lemon (see page 68) and a pinch of dried sage. Cover and cook over a medium heat for 8–10 minutes until just tender. Season and serve with tagines.

20 Carrot, Potato and Sage Tagine

Heat 2 tablespoons argan oil or ghee in a heavy-based frying pan or the base of a tagine, stir in 2–3 crushed garlic cloves, 1 teaspoon coriander seeds and 1 tablespoon crumbled dried sage and cook for 1–2 minutes. Toss in 2 peeled and thickly sliced carrots and 4 peeled and thickly sliced potatoes. Stir in 2 teaspoons turmeric, 1 teaspoon smoked paprika, 1 tablespoon runny honey and the juice of 2 lemons. Season, re-cover and cook gently for 15 minutes until the vegetables are tender. Serve as a side dish.

Three Pepper, Olive, Feta and Egg Tagine

Serves 4

2 tablespoons olive oil

1 teaspoon cumin seeds

1 teaspoon coriander seeds

1 green, red and yellow pepper, all cored, deseeded and finely sliced

2 tablespoons pitted and halved black olives

150 g (5 oz) feta cheese, cubed

4 eggs

pepper

shredded basil leaves, to garnish

chunks of warm crusty bread, to serve (optional)

- Heat the oil in a heavy-based frying pan or the base of a tagine, stir in the cumin and coriander seeds and cook for 1–2 minutes. Add the peppers and cook for a further 2–3 minutes, then stir in the olives. Cover, reduce the heat and cook over a medium heat for 5 minutes until the peppers have softened.

- Add the feta and cook for 2–3 minutes until it begins to soften, then make 4 wells in the mixture. Break the eggs into the wells, cover and cook for 4–5 minutes until the whites are firm. Grind pepper over the eggs, garnish with the basil leaves and serve with warm crusty bread, if liked.

 Spiced Tomatoes and Eggs with Roasted Red Peppers

Heat 1–2 tablespoons ghee in a heavy-based frying pan or the base of a tagine, stir in 1 teaspoon each of coriander seeds and cumin seeds and 2 crushed garlic cloves and cook for 1–2 minutes. Top with 3–4 sliced tomatoes, then break over 8 eggs. Cover and cook over a medium heat for 6–8 minutes until the eggs are firm. Season, garnish with roasted red peppers from a jar, sliced, and scatter over a chopped small bunch of flat leaf parsley. Serve on buttered, toasted flatbreads.

 Pepper, Tomato and Egg Tagine

Heat 2 tablespoons ghee in a heavy-based frying pan or the base of a tagine, stir in 2–3 chopped garlic cloves, 1–2 teaspoons coriander seeds, 1 teaspoon cumin seeds and 2 deseeded and finely sliced red chillies and cook for 2 minutes. Add 2 finely sliced onions and 2 cored, deseeded and finely sliced red or green peppers and cook for 2–3 minutes to soften, then stir in 1–2 teaspoons sugar and a 400 g (13 oz) can chopped tomatoes. Cover and cook over a medium heat for 15–20 minutes until thickened. Make 4–6 wells in the mixture, then break 4–6 eggs into the wells, re-cover and cook gently for 4–5 minutes until the whites are firm. Scatter over a finely chopped small bunch of flat leaf parsley and serve with dollops of yogurt and chunks of crusty bread.

30 Spicy Courgette, Aubergine and Date Tagine

Serves 4

3–4 tablespoons olive oil

2–3 garlic cloves, chopped

1 onion, sliced

1 red pepper, cored, deseeded and sliced

1 aubergine, halved and sliced

2 courgettes, sliced

225 g (7½ oz) ready-to-eat pitted dates, halved lengthways

2–3 teaspoons ras el hanout

2 teaspoons sugar

2 x 400 g (13 oz) cans chopped tomatoes

bunch of flat leaf parsley, chopped

small bunch of coriander, chopped

salt and pepper

To serve

natural yogurt

chunks of crusty bread

- Heat the oil in a heavy-based frying pan or the base of a tagine, stir in the garlic, onion and red pepper and cook for 1 minute, then add the aubergine and courgettes and cook for a further 2 minutes.

- Add the dates, ras el hanout, sugar, tomatoes and half the herbs and heat until bubbling for 2 minutes. Cover and cook over a medium heat for 25 minutes.

- Season, garnish with the remaining herbs and serve with dollops of yogurt and crusty bread.

---

1 Spicy Courgettes, Apricots and Dates

Heat 2 tablespoons olive oil and a knob of butter in a frying pan or tagine, stir in 2–3 sliced courgettes and cook for 4–5 minutes. Slice and add 1 tablespoon each of dried apricots and pitted dates with 1 teaspoon dried red chilli and 2 tablespoons orange blossom water. Season, cover and cook for 4–5 minutes more. Garnish with the sliced rind of ½ preserved lemon (see page 68) and serve as a side dish.

2 Ras el Hanout Courgette and Aubergine Tagine

Heat 4 tablespoons olive or argan oil in a heavy-based frying pan or the base of a tagine, stir in 2–3 crushed garlic cloves and cook for 1 minute. Add 1 diced aubergine and 2 diced courgettes and cook for 2–3 minutes to soften. Add 2 teaspoons ras el hanout, 2 teaspoons sugar, 1 tablespoon finely chopped coriander and a 400 g (13 oz) can chopped tomatoes. Bring to the boil, then cover and cook over a medium heat for 15 minutes. Garnish with a little more finely chopped coriander mixed with the finely chopped rind of ½ preserved lemon (see page 68) and serve as a side dish.

10 Simple Harissa Beans

Serves 4

2 tablespoons olive oil

2 garlic cloves, finely chopped

1 finely chopped onion

2 teaspoons cumin seeds

1 teaspoon sugar

2 teaspoons harissa paste
(see page 70)

450 g (14½ oz) canned kidney
beans, rinsed and drained

juice of 1 lemon

small bunch of coriander,
finely chopped

salt and pepper

- Heat the oil in a heavy-based frying pan or the base of a tagine, stir in the garlic, onion, cumin seeds and sugar and cook for 2–3 minutes until they begin to colour.

- Add the harissa, kidney beans and lemon juice, cover and cook gently for 4–5 minutes until heated through. Season and stir in the coriander. Serve as a side dish.

 Harissa, Bean and Olive Tagine

Heat 2 tablespoons olive oil in a frying pan or tagine, stir in 2 chopped garlic cloves, the sliced rind of 1 preserved lemon (see page 68) and 1 teaspoon coriander seeds and cook for 1–2 minutes. Add 450 g (14½ oz) canned butter beans, rinsed and drained, and mix well, then add 2 tablespoons pitted black olives. Stir in 1 teaspoon sugar, 1–2 teaspoons harissa paste (see page 70) and a 400 g (13 oz) can chopped tomatoes. Bring to the boil, then cover and cook over a medium heat for 15 minutes. Season and stir in a chopped bunch each of flat leaf parsley and mint. Garnish with more chopped mint and serve with crusty bread.

 Harissa Bean Tagine

Heat 2 tablespoons ghee or olive oil with a knob of butter in a heavy-based frying pan or the base of a tagine, stir in 2 finely chopped garlic cloves and 1 finely chopped onion and cook for 2–3 minutes. Add 1 teaspoon each of ground fenugreek and sugar and stir in 1–2 teaspoons harissa paste (see page 70) and 2 teaspoons tomato purée. Toss in a 400 g (13 oz) can haricot or soya beans, rinsed and drained, and mix well. Pour in just enough water to cover the beans, bring to the boil, cover and cook over a gentle heat for 25 minutes, or until tender. Season, toss in half of a finely chopped small bunch each of flat leaf parsley and coriander and garnish with the rest. Serve with yogurt, pickles and flatbreads.

10 Ras el Hanout Lentils and Chickpeas

Serves 4

2 tablespoons ghee or butter

2 garlic cloves, crushed

1 tablespoon peeled and finely chopped fresh root ginger

250 g (8 oz) pouch ready-cooked brown lentils

150 g (5 oz) canned chickpeas, rinsed and drained

2 tablespoons pine nuts

1 teaspoon ras el hanout

small bunch of coriander, finely chopped

salt

couscous, to serve

- Heat 1 tablespoon of the ghee or butter in a heavy-based frying pan or the base of a tagine, stir in the garlic and ginger and cook for 2 minutes. Add the lentils and chickpeas and cook for a further 2–3 minutes, then season with salt.

- Meanwhile, in a separate heavy-based frying pan, dry-fry the pine nuts over a medium heat for 2–3 minutes until they emit a nutty aroma. Stir in the remaining ghee or butter and the ras el hanout.

- Pour the pine nut mixture over the lentils and chickpeas, toss well and sprinkle with the coriander. Serve spooned over couscous as a side dish.

 Green Lentil and Ras el Hanout Tagine Heat 2 tablespoons ghee or argan oil in a heavy-based frying pan or the base of a tagine, stir in 2–3 crushed garlic cloves and 1 teaspoon caraway seeds and cook for 1 minute. Stir in 1 finely chopped onion, 1 peeled and finely diced carrot and 1 teaspoon sugar and cook for 2–3 minutes. Add 1–2 teaspoons ras el hanout and 225 g (7½ oz) green lentils, which have been soaked for at least 6 hours and drained. Pour in enough water to cover the lentils by 2.5 cm (1 inch) and bring to the boil. Cover and cook over a medium heat for 15 minutes until the water has been absorbed and the lentils are tender. Season well, garnish with a finely chopped small bunch of flat leaf parsley and serve with yogurt and pickles.

 Lentil, Ginger and Ras el Hanout Tagine Heat 2 tablespoons ghee in a frying pan or tagine, stir in 1 chopped onion, 4 chopped garlic cloves and 50 g (2 oz) fresh root ginger, peeled and chopped, and cook for 2–3 minutes. Stir in 2–3 teaspoons ras el hanout, 1 teaspoon sugar and 250 g (8 oz) brown lentils, picked over, rinsed and drained, and mix well. Add 700 ml (1¼ pints) hot water, stir well and bring to the boil. Cover, reduce the heat and cook gently for 25 minutes until all the liquid has been absorbed and the lentils are tender. Season, stir in a little of a bunch of coriander, then garnish with the rest. Serve with yogurt and pickles or preserves.

30 Saffron, Onion, Chicken, Turnip and Chickpea K'dra

Serves 6–8

2–3 tablespoons smen or ghee
4 onions, finely chopped
2 teaspoons cumin seeds
2–3 cinnamon sticks
pinch of saffron threads
12 chicken thighs, skinned
450 g (14½ oz) canned chickpeas,
  rinsed and drained
1.2 litres (2 pints) hot chicken stock
450 g (14½ oz) peeled turnips,
  cut into bite-sized chunks
2 tablespoons sultanas
1 teaspoon sea salt
1 teaspoon freshly ground
  black pepper
½ tablespoon butter
bunch of flat leaf parsley,
  finely chopped
couscous, to serve (optional)

- Heat the smen or ghee in a large copper or heavy-based saucepan, stir in the onions, cumin seeds, cinnamon sticks and saffron and cook for 1–2 minutes. Add the chicken and coat well, then add the chickpeas. Pour in the stock and bring to the boil, then reduce the heat and cook over a medium heat for 15 minutes.

- Add the turnips and sultanas, re-cover and cook over a medium heat for a further 10 minutes until the chicken is cooked through. Season with the salt and pepper and stir in the butter and parsley. Serve the chicken, chickpeas and turnip with couscous, if liked, pouring the sauce into a bowl to serve separately.

 Saffron Onions and Sultanas

Heat 1–2 tablespoons smen or ghee in a heavy-based saucepan or the base of a tagine, stir in 3–4 finely sliced or chopped onions and cook for 1–2 minutes to soften. Add 2 tablespoons sultanas and a pinch of saffron threads, cover and cook gently for 8 minutes. Season with a little salt and serve the onion mixture as a side dish with k'dras or couscous.

 Quick Saffron, Onion, Sultana and Chicken K'dra with Spicy Couscous Heat 2 tablespoons smen or ghee in a large copper or heavy-based saucepan, stir in 3 finely sliced onions, 2 deseeded and finely sliced red chillies, 2 teaspoons coriander seeds and a pinch of saffron threads and cook for 2–3 minutes. Add 500 g (1 lb) finely sliced or diced chicken breast fillets and mix well, then stir in 2 tablespoons sultanas. Pour in enough chicken stock to just cover the chicken and bring to the boil. Cover and cook over a medium heat for 15 minutes until the chicken is cooked through. Season and stir in ½ tablespoon butter or smen and the finely sliced rind of ½ preserved lemon (see page 68). Serve with spicy couscous.

QuickCook

Grills,
Roasts and
Pan-Fries

Recipes listed by cooking time

30

20

Moroccan Onion and Lamb Kebabs

Serves 4

2 large onions
1 teaspoon salt
2 teaspoons ras el hanout
2 tablespoons olive oil
juice of 1 lemon
500 g (1 lb) lamb shoulder,
    cut into bite-sized chunks
bunch of flat leaf parsley,
    trimmed
lemon wedges, to serve

- Grate the onions into a large bowl, sprinkle with the salt and leave to stand for 5 minutes. Tightly squeeze the onion into a non-metallic bowl to extract the juice, then discard the grated onion.

- Stir the ras el hanout into the onion juice with the oil and lemon juice. Toss in the lamb and coat well, then leave to marinate for 15 minutes.

- Thread the marinated lamb on to 4 metal skewers and cook over a barbecue or under a preheated grill for 3–4 minutes on each side until cooked through. Arrange the cooked kebabs on a flat serving dish, garnish with the parsley and serve with lemon wedges to squeeze over.

 Grilled Lamb Steaks with Peppers and Onions Lightly brush 4 lamb steaks, about 150 g (5 oz) each, with a little olive oil and season. Cook under a preheated medium-hot grill for 3–4 minutes on each side until cooked through. Meanwhile, heat 2 tablespoons olive or argan oil in a heavy-based frying pan, stir in 1 finely sliced onion, 1 cored, deseeded and finely sliced red or green pepper and 1 teaspoon sugar and cook for 3–4 minutes. Toss in the finely chopped rind of ½ preserved lemon (see page 68), season well and serve with the cooked steaks.

 Lamb, Pepper and Onion Kebabs Put 450 g (14½ oz) lean lamb, cut into bite-sized chunks, in a non-metallic bowl and toss with 2 tablespoons olive oil, the juice of 1 lemon, 2 crushed garlic cloves and 1 teaspoon crushed cumin seeds. Leave to marinate for 10 minutes. Core, deseed and cut 2 red or green peppers into bite-sized pieces and chop 1 onion into bite-sized pieces. Thread the lamb onto 4 metal skewers, alternating with the peppers and onion, then cook over a barbecue or under a preheated grill for 3–4 minutes on each side until cooked through. Season and serve with couscous and pickles.

MOR-GRIL-WYR

1 Moroccan Onion and Cumin Beef Burgers

Serves 4

450 g (14½ oz) lean minced beef
1 onion, finely chopped
2 garlic cloves, crushed
2 teaspoons cumin seeds, crushed
1 teaspoon harissa paste
(see page 70)
small bunch of flat leaf parsley,
finely chopped
olive oil, for brushing
salt and pepper

To serve

flatbreads
Moroccan pickles or chutneys

- Place the beef, onion, garlic, cumin seeds, harissa and parsley in a bowl and season well. Knead the mixture well, lifting it up and slapping it back into the bowl until slightly sticky, then divide into 8 pieces and shape into firm patties.

- Lightly brush the patties with a little oil and cook over a barbecue or under a preheated hot grill for 3–4 minutes on each side until cooked through. Serve with flatbreads and Moroccan pickles or chutneys.

---

 2 Chargrilled Onion and Cumin Beef Kebabs Place 450 g (14½ oz) minced beef, 1 chopped onion, 2 crushed garlic cloves, 2 teaspoons ground cumin, 1 teaspoon cayenne powder and a chopped small bunch of parsley in a bowl and season well. Knead the mixture as above, then divide into 4 and mould around 4 metal skewers. Brush with a little olive oil and cook over a barbecue or under a preheated grill for 4–5 minutes on each side until cooked through. Toast 4 flatbreads for 1–2 minutes, then slit open. Slide the kebabs into the hollows and divide a bunch of coriander leaves among them. Serve with harissa paste (see page 70) and yogurt.

 3 Onion and Cumin Beef Kebabs with Chickpea Purée Put a 400 g (13 oz) can chickpeas, rinsed and drained, 2–3 tablespoons olive oil, the juice of 1 lemon, 1 garlic clove and 1 teaspoon ground cumin into a food processor and whizz to a thick paste. Add 2 tablespoons natural yogurt, season and whizz again, then tip the mixture into an ovenproof dish. Drizzle over 1 tablespoon melted butter or ghee and place in a preheated oven, 180°C (350°F), Gas Mark 4, for 15 minutes until lightly browned. Meanwhile, mix together 450 g (14½ oz) lean finely minced beef, 1 grated onion and 2 teaspoons toasted and ground cumin seeds in a bowl. Add 1 teaspoon caraway seeds, 1 teaspoon smoked paprika, ½ teaspoon cayenne or chilli powder and a finely chopped small bunch each of flat leaf parsley and coriander and season well. Knead the mixture as above for 1–2 minutes until smooth and slightly sticky. Divide into 4 and mould around 4 metal skewers. Lightly brush with olive or sunflower oil, then cook over a barbecue or under a preheated grill for 4–5 minutes on each side, or until cooked through. Garnish with extra herbs and serve immediately with the hot chickpea purée.

MOR-GRIL-BOH

30 Fennel-Roasted Lamb Fillet with Honeyed Figs

Serves 4

3 garlic cloves, chopped
25 g (1 oz) fresh root ginger,
  peeled and chopped
1 red chilli, deseeded and chopped
1 teaspoon sea salt
1 teaspoon ground coriander
1 teaspoon ground cumin
2 tablespoons smen, ghee or
  softened butter
2 teaspoons fennel seeds
700 g (1½ lb) lean lamb fillet or loin
4 fresh figs, halved or quartered
2 tablespoons runny honey
salt and pepper
small bunch of coriander, finely
  chopped, to garnish
couscous, to serve (optional)

- Using a pestle and mortar, pound the garlic, ginger, chilli and salt to form a coarse paste, then add the ground spices. Beat the paste into the smen, ghee or butter with the fennel seeds.

- Cut small incisions in the lamb and rub the mixture all over the meat, pressing it into the incisions. Place the lamb in a roasting tin and roast in a preheated oven, 200 °C (400 °F), Gas Mark 6, for 15 minutes.

- Baste the lamb with the cooking juices, arrange the figs around it and drizzle with honey. Season, then return to the oven and cook for a further 10 minutes until cooked through. Garnish with the chopped coriander and serve thickly sliced, with couscous, if liked.

---

1 Roasted Fennel and Honey Figs

Cut 8 fresh figs into quarters, keeping the bases intact, and place in an ovenproof dish. Dab a little smen or butter into each one, scatter over 1 teaspoon fennel seeds and drizzle with 1–2 tablespoons runny honey. Place in a preheated oven, 200 °C (400 °F), Gas Mark 6, for 8 minutes until softened and the honey has melted. Serve with grilled and roasted meats.

2 Honey and Fennel-Roasted

Lamb Steaks Put 1 tablespoon smen, ghee or softened butter into a bowl and beat in 2 crushed garlic cloves and 2 teaspoons crushed fennel seeds, then season. Cut 500 g (1 lb) lamb fillet or loin into 4 steaks and place in a roasting tin. Rub over the fennel mixture and place in a preheated oven, 200 °C (400 °F), Gas Mark 6, for 15 minutes until cooked through, turning them over halfway through and drizzling with 1 tablespoon runny honey. Serve the lamb with the juices spooned over and lemon wedges to squeeze over.

Spicy Chargrilled Meatballs with Toasted Coconut

Serves 4

1 teaspoon cumin seeds
1 teaspoon coriander seeds
4 tablespoons desiccated or
   freshly grated coconut
350 g (11½ oz) lean minced beef
1 small onion, finely chopped
2 garlic cloves, finely chopped
1 red chilli, deseeded and chopped
1 teaspoon ground cinnamon
salt and pepper
small bunch of coriander,
   finely chopped, to garnish

To serve
pitta breads
lime wedges`

- Dry-fry the seeds in a small, heavy-based frying pan over a medium heat for 1–2 minutes until they emit a nutty aroma. Using a pestle and mortar or a spice grinder, grind to a powder. Dry-fry the coconut for 1–2 minutes until it begins to colour, then tip onto a plate to cool.

- Mix together the beef, onion, garlic, chilli, cinnamon, ground spices and 3 tablespoons of the coconut and season well. Knead the mixture well for 1–2 minutes. Cover and chill for 10 minutes.

- Knead the mixture and roll into small balls. Thread on to 4 large or 8 small metal skewers and cook over a barbecue or under a preheated grill for 3–4 minutes on each side until cooked through. Sprinkle with the remaining coconut and the chopped coriander and serve with pittas, with lime wedges to squeeze over.

---

10 Pan-Fried Spiced Coconut and Dried Fruit Dry-fry 1 teaspoon each of cumin, coriander, fennel and cardamom seeds in a large, heavy-based frying pan over a medium heat for 1 minute. Add 2–3 tablespoons finely sliced dried or fresh coconut for 1–2 minutes until it emits a nutty aroma. Stir in 1 heaped tablespoon ghee or butter until melted, then stir in 2 tablespoons each of finely sliced ready-to-eat pitted dates and dried apricots for 2–3 minutes. Sprinkle with 1 teaspoon ground cinnamon and a little salt. Serve hot with couscous or grilled lamb.

20 Chargrilled Coconut and Chilli Meatballs Mix together 250 g (8 oz) lean minced lamb, 1 finely chopped onion, 2 crushed garlic cloves, 1 deseeded and finely chopped red chilli, 2 tablespoons desiccated coconut and 2 teaspoons ground cinnamon in a bowl and season. Knead the mixture well and roll into small balls, then thread onto 4 large or 8 small metal skewers. Brush with a little olive oil and cook over a barbecue or under a preheated grill for 3–4 minutes on each side until cooked through. Serve with lemon wedges to squeeze over.

MOR-GRIL-RYO

30 Spicy Pan-Fried Liver, Prunes and Onions

Serves 4

350 g (11½ oz) lambs' or ox liver,
  trimmed and thinly sliced
2 tablespoons plain flour
4 tablespoons ghee, smen or
  argan oil
2 teaspoons cumin seeds
1 teaspoon coriander seeds
1 teaspoon fennel seeds
6 cloves
2 cinnamon sticks
2 garlic cloves, finely chopped
1 red chilli, deseeded and sliced
2 red onions, finely sliced
175 g (6 oz) ready-to-eat pitted
  dried prunes, finely sliced
2 tablespoons chopped coriander
4 flatbreads
butter or ghee, for spreading
salt and pepper
4 tablespoons yogurt, to serve

- Toss the liver in the flour. Heat 2 tablespoons of the ghee, smen or oil in a heavy-based frying pan, add the liver and cook for 3–4 minutes until browned all over and just cooked through. Season, then drain on kitchen paper and set aside.

- Dry-fry the seeds in a heavy-based frying pan over a medium heat for 1–2 minutes until they emit a nutty aroma. Stir in the remaining ghee, smen or oil and add the cloves, cinnamon, garlic, chilli and onions and cook for 4–5 minutes until the onions are softened and beginning to brown.

- Add the prunes and cook for 1 minute, then add the chopped coriander and liver and heat through for 3–4 minutes, stirring to coat well, then season.

- Meanwhile, lightly toast the flatbreads, spread with a little butter or ghee and place on 4 serving plates. Spoon the liver and prunes on top of each and serve with dollops of yogurt.

 Quick Pan-Fried Spicy Lambs' Liver

Heat 2 tablespoons olive or argan oil in a frying pan, stir in 2 chopped garlic cloves, 1 deseeded and chopped red chilli and 1–2 teaspoons cumin seeds and cook for 2 minutes. Toss in 350 g (11½ oz) trimmed, sliced and floured lambs' liver and cook for 3–4 minutes. Season and stir in 1–2 tablespoons chopped coriander. Spoon onto toasted flatbreads and serve with lemon wedges.

 Liver Kebabs with Coriander Onions

Heat 2 tablespoons ghee or argan oil in a heavy-based frying pan, stir in 2 finely sliced onions and 1 teaspoon sugar and cook for 3–4 minutes until softened and golden brown. Toss in 2 tablespoons finely chopped coriander and season. Cover and keep warm. Cut 250 g (8 oz) trimmed lambs' liver into bite-sized cubes and thread on to 4 large or 8 small metal skewers, alternating with 2 thinly sliced merguez or chorizo sausages. Lightly brush with a little olive oil and cook under a preheated hot grill for 2–3 minutes on each side until cooked through. Season and serve with the coriander onions.

MOR-GRIL-HAK

Roasted Cinnamon Chicken Thighs and Plums

Serves 4

2 tablespoons olive or argan oil

15 g (½ oz) butter

8 chicken thighs

2 teaspoons coriander seeds

4 cinnamon sticks

2–3 dried red chillies

75 ml (3 fl oz) white wine,
  chicken stock or water

4–6 sweet plums, halved
  and stoned

1 tablespoon runny honey

1 teaspoon ground cinnamon

salt and pepper

couscous or chunks of crusty
  bread, to serve (optional)

· Heat the oil and butter in a large, heavy-based frying pan, add the chicken thighs and brown for 2–3 minutes, turning once. Place in an ovenproof dish, pour over the butter and oil and scatter the coriander seeds, cinnamon sticks and chillies over and around them. Pour in the wine, stock or water and season.

· Place in a preheated oven, 180°C (350°F), Gas Mark 4, for 15 minutes. Arrange the plums around the chicken, drizzle with the honey and sprinkle over the ground cinnamon. Return to the oven and cook for a further 10 minutes until the chicken is cooked through. Serve with couscous or crusty bread, if liked.

 Grilled Cinnamon Chicken with Plum Sauce Cut 3 skinless chicken breast fillets, about 150 g (5 oz) each, into 3–4 long pieces each and lightly brush with sunflower or olive oil. Cook under a preheated medium-hot grill for 2–3 minutes, then turn the chicken over, brush lightly with more oil and cook for a further 2–3 minutes until cooked through. Dust with 1–2 teaspoons ground cinnamon, season and serve with ready-made plum sauce for dipping.

Pan-Fried Cinnamon Chicken and Plums Heat 2 tablespoons ghee or argan oil in a large, heavy-based frying pan, stir in 2–3 finely chopped garlic cloves, 1 finely chopped onion, 25 g (1 oz) fresh root ginger, peeled and finely chopped, 1 teaspoon finely chopped dried red chilli, 2 teaspoons fennel seeds and 1 teaspoon sugar and cook for 2–3 minutes until the onion softens and begins to colour. Add 175 g (6 oz) skinless chicken breast fillets, cut into bite-sized chunks, and stir to coat well. Cover and cook over a medium heat, stirring occasionally, for 8–10 minutes. Season and add 3 stoned and quartered plums and 1–2 teaspoons ground cinnamon. Cover and cook for a further 5 minutes until the chicken is cooked through. Garnish with a little finely chopped coriander and serve with couscous.

30 Roasted Honeyed Quince and Duck Legs

Serves 4

4 duck legs
3 tablespoons olive oil
25 g (1 oz) butter
25 g (1 oz) fresh root ginger,
   peeled and finely chopped
1 large quince, cut into
   8 segments
juice of 1 lemon
2 tablespoons runny honey
2 teaspoons ground cinnamon
salt and pepper
small bunch of coriander,
   finely chopped, to garnish
couscous, to serve (optional)

- Rub the duck legs with 2 tablespoons of the oil, season and place in a roasting tin. Place in a preheated oven, 200°C (400°F), Gas Mark 6, for 20 minutes.

- Meanwhile, heat the remaining oil and the butter in a heavy-based frying pan, stir in the ginger and cook for 1 minute. Add the quince segments and cook for 2–3 minutes on each side until they are golden brown. Turn off the heat and pour over the lemon juice.

- Pour off any excess fat from the duck legs and arrange the pieces of quince around them. Drizzle the honey over the duck and quince and sprinkle over the cinnamon. Return to the oven and cook for a further 10 minutes until the duck legs are cooked through. Garnish with the coriander and serve with couscous, if liked.

 Chargrilled Honey and Sesame Duck Skewers Thread 175 g (6 oz) skinless duck breast fillets, cut into thin strips, onto 4 large or 8 small metal skewers. Sprinkle with a little salt and cook over a barbecue or under a preheated grill for 2–3 minutes on each side until just cooked through. Place on a plate and drizzle with 2 tablespoons warmed honey, then roll in a bowl of toasted sesame seeds. Serve at once.

 Pan-Fried Duck, Almond and Honey Rice Pour 600 ml (1 pint) water or chicken stock into a large saucepan and bring to the boil. Stir in 200 g (7 oz) rinsed and drained long grain rice with 1 teaspoon salt. Bring back to the boil, then cook over a medium heat for about 10 minutes until the water has been absorbed. Turn off the heat, cover the pan with a clean tea towel, put on the lid and leave to steam for 5 minutes. Meanwhile, heat 2 tablespoons ghee or olive oil in a large, heavy-based frying pan, stir in 1 finely chopped onion, 2 finely chopped garlic cloves and 2 teaspoons fennel seeds and cook for 1–2 minutes. Add 2 tablespoons finely sliced blanched almonds and 175 g (6 oz) diced skinless duck breast fillets and cook for 3–4 minutes until just cooked through. Add 2 teaspoons ras el hanout and season. When ready, add the rice to the pan and mix well. Drizzle with 1–2 tablespoons runny honey, dust with 1 teaspoon ground cinnamon and serve with yogurt and pickles.

MOR-GRIL-ZUT

30 Pan-Fried Quails with Ginger and Grapes

Serves 4

2 tablespoons sunflower oil
50 g (2 oz) butter
4–6 oven-ready quails
50 g (2 oz) fresh root ginger,
   peeled and finely chopped
3 garlic cloves, finely chopped
250 g (8 oz) seedless green or
   red grapes, halved
salt and pepper
couscous, to serve

- Heat the oil and most of the butter in large, heavy-based frying pan. Add the quails and brown on both sides for 4–5 minutes, then transfer to a plate.

- Stir the ginger and garlic into the pan, cook for 1–2 minutes, then toss in the grapes and season well. Return the quails to the pan, cover and cook over a medium heat for 20 minutes, or until cooked through. Serve with couscous.

---

10 **Pan-Fried Quails' Eggs with Ginger**
Heat 1–2 tablespoons ghee or butter in a heavy-based frying pan, stir in 12 shop-bought shelled hard-boiled quails' eggs and cook for 2–3 minutes. Season and dust with 1 teaspoon ground ginger. Serve hot with a dab of harissa paste (see page 70).

20 **Roasted Quails with Ginger and Grapes** Whisk together the juice of 1 lemon and 2 tablespoons olive oil in a small bowl, then rub over 4–6 plucked and cleaned quails. Season and place in a roasting tin or ovenproof dish. Peel and cut 25 g (1 oz) fresh root ginger into matchsticks, scatter around the quail and

drizzle over a little more olive oil. Place in a preheated oven, 190°C (375°F), Gas Mark 5, for 10 minutes. Add 2–3 tablespoons halved seedless grapes and mix well with the root ginger. Return to the oven and cook for a further 5–6 minutes, or until the quails are cooked through and lightly browned.

MOR-GRIL-HAE

3⬤ Chargrilled Harissa Chicken Wings with Burnt Oranges

Serves 4

1 tablespoon harissa paste
  (see page 70)
2 tablespoons olive oil
small bunch of coriander,
  finely chopped
8–12 chicken wings
salt
small bunch of flat leaf parsley,
  roughly chopped, to garnish

For the oranges

2 oranges, cut into quarters
2 tablespoons icing sugar

- In a bowl, beat the harissa into the oil, season with salt and stir in the coriander. Put the chicken wings into a dish and brush over the harissa oil. Cover and leave to marinate for 15 minutes.

- Cook the marinated wings over a hot barbecue or under a preheated hot grill, basting with any remaining harissa oil, for 3–4 minutes on each side until cooked through.

- Meanwhile, dip the oranges into the icing sugar and cook over the barbecue or under a preheated hot grill for about 2–3 minutes on each side until slightly burned but not black.

- Serve the chicken and oranges garnished with the parsley.

 Grilled Dukkah Chicken and Oranges with Harissa Dip
Brush 8 chicken wings with a little olive oil and toss in 2–3 tablespoons ready-made dukkah spice mix. Cook under a preheated medium grill with 1 orange, cut into wedges, for 3–4 minutes on each side until cooked through. Meanwhile, mix together 2 tablespoons olive oil, the juice of ½ lemon and 2 teaspoons harissa paste (see page 70) in a small bowl. Serve the dip with the chicken and oranges.

 Grilled Harissa Chicken with Dukkah Orange Dip In a small bowl, mix together 2 teaspoons harissa paste (see page 70), 2 teaspoons runny honey and 1 tablespoon olive oil to form a smooth paste. Smear it over 8 chicken wings, then cover and leave to marinate for 10 minutes. Meanwhile, whisk together 2 tablespoons olive oil and the juice of 1 orange, then stir in 2 tablespoons dukkah spice mix (for homemade, see page 118). Cook the chicken under a preheated medium grill for

3–4 minutes on each side until cooked through. Serve immediately with the dukkah dip.

MOR-GRIL-WEB

Chicken Livers and Pomegranate Syrup on Fried Bread

Serves 4

2–3 tablespoons olive or argan oil
15 g (½ oz) butter
4 slices of crusty bread
2–3 garlic cloves, finely chopped
1 dried red chilli, finely chopped
1 teaspoon cumin seeds
1 teaspoon coriander seeds
450 g (14½ oz) chicken livers,
  trimmed and cut into chunks
2 tablespoons pomegranate syrup
salt and pepper

To garnish

finely sliced or chopped rind of
  ½ preserved lemon (see page 68)
small bunch of flat leaf parsley,
  finely chopped

- Heat the oil and butter in a heavy-based frying pan, add the bread slices and fry for 2–3 minutes on each side until crisp and golden brown. Drain on kitchen paper and set aside.

- Stir the garlic, chilli and seeds into the pan and cook for 2 minutes. Add the chicken livers and cook, stirring, for 3–4 minutes until browned all over. Season and stir in the pomegranate syrup.

- Place the fried bread on a serving dish and spoon over the chicken livers. Garnish with the preserved lemon rind and parsley and serve.

 Pan-Fried Chicken Livers and Pomegranate Syrup Trim and chop 350 g (11½ oz) chicken livers. Heat 2 tablespoons olive or argan oil and a little butter in a heavy-based frying pan, stir in 2 crushed garlic cloves and 1 teaspoon coriander seeds and cook for 1–2 minutes. Toss in the chicken livers and cook for 3–4 minutes until browned all over, then stir in 1 tablespoon pomegranate syrup and season. Garnish with 2 teaspoons finely chopped preserved lemon rind (see page 68) and serve on toasted flatbreads.

 Chicken Liver and Pomegranate Syrup Rice Heat 1 tablespoon ghee in a heavy-based saucepan, stir in 1 finely chopped onion, 4–6 cloves and 1 teaspoon sugar and cook for 2–3 minutes until the onion begins to colour. Stir in 200 g (7 oz) rinsed and drained long grain rice, season and pour in 600 ml (1 pint) water. Bring to the boil and cook for 2–3 minutes, then reduce the heat and cook gently for 10–12 minutes until the water has been absorbed. Turn off the heat, cover the pan with a clean tea towel, put on the lid and leave to steam for 5–8 minutes. While the rice is steaming, heat 2 tablespoons ghee or smen in a separate heavy-based saucepan, stir in 1 finely chopped onion, 2 finely chopped garlic cloves, 1 teaspoon each of cumin seeds and coriander seeds and cook for 2–3 minutes. Add 250 g (8 oz) trimmed and diced chicken livers, coat well and cook for 3–4 minutes until they are browned all over, then stir in 1 tablespoon pomegranate syrup. Add the rice to the pan and mix well. Serve garnished with a finely chopped small bunch of coriander.

MOR-GRIL-KEK

3 Grilled Red Mullet Fillets with Chermoula Sauce

Serves 4

4 whole red mullet, about 125 g
(4 oz) each
oil, for greasing
small bunch of flat leaf parsley,
roughly chopped, to garnish
couscous, to serve

For the chermoula sauce

1 teaspoon saffron threads
2 teaspoons water
2–3 garlic cloves, chopped
1 red chilli, deseeded and chopped
1–2 teaspoons cumin seeds
1 teaspoon sea salt
4 tablespoons olive oil
juice of 1 lemon
small bunch of coriander,
finely chopped
pepper

- To make the sauce, place the saffron in a small bowl with the measurement water and leave to soak for 5 minutes. Using a pestle and mortar, pound the garlic, chilli, cumin seeds and salt to form a coarse paste. Gradually whisk in the oil and lemon juice, then stir in the coriander and season with pepper. Tip in the saffron water and mix well.

- Make 3–4 slashes on both sides of each fish, place on an oiled grill pan and brush with a little of the sauce. Cook under a preheated hot grill for 4–5 minutes, then turn, brush with a little more sauce and cook for 3–4 minutes, or until cooked through.

- Meanwhile, heat the remaining sauce in a small saucepan. Place the fish in a serving dish, spoon over the sauce and garnish with the parsley. Serve with couscous.

 Chargrilled Red Mullet with Chermoula Rinse and pat dry 4 gutted red mullet, about 250–300 g (8–10 oz) each and brush with a litte melted ghee on one side of each fish. Cook over a barbecue or under a preheated grill for 3–4 minutes on each side, brushing with melted ghee when you turn the fish over. When cooked through, sprinkle with 1–2 teaspoons sumac and serve with shop-bought ready-made chermoula paste.

 Griddled Red Mullet with Chermoula Dressing Rinse and pat dry 4 gutted red mullet, about 250–300 g (8–10 oz) each, and season. Using a pestle and mortar, pound 2 chopped garlic cloves, 1 deseeded and chopped green chilli, 1 teaspoon coriander seeds and a little sea salt to form a coarse paste. Whisk in 1 tablespoon olive oil, the juice of 1 lemon and 1 tablespoon finely chopped coriander. Set the dressing aside. Rinse and drain 2 handfuls of rocket leaves and arrange on a serving dish. Heat 1 tablespoon olive oil in a griddle or heavy-based frying pan, tipping the pan to spread the oil over the base. Add the fish and cook for 4–5 minutes on each side, or until cooked through. Place on the rocket leaves and drizzle over the chermoula dressing.

Roasted Chilli and Preserved Lemon Sardines

Serves 4

3 garlic cloves, finely sliced

2 red chillies, deseeded and finely sliced

finely sliced rind of 1 preserved lemon (see page 68)

3 tablespoons olive or argan oil

juice of 1 lemon

salt and pepper

8 sardines, gutted and cleaned

small bunch of flat leaf parsley, finely chopped, to garnish

chunks of crusty bread, to serve (optional)

- Mix together the garlic, chillies and preserved lemon rind in a bowl, then mix in the oil and lemon juice and season well.

- Spread some of the mixture over the base of an ovenproof dish. Put the sardines on top and spoon over the remaining mixture. Place in a preheated oven, 200 °C (400 °F), Gas Mark 6, for 10–15 minutes, or until the sardines are cooked.

- Transfer the sardines to a serving dish, spoon over the juices and garnish with the parsley. Serve with crusty bread, if liked.

 Chargrilled Tabil and Preserved Lemon Sardines Rinse and pat dry 4–8 gutted sardines. Melt 2 tablespoons ghee in a small saucepan, then stir in 2 teaspoons tabil spice mix and the finely chopped rind of ½ preserved lemon (see page 68). Brush the sardines with the ghee and season well. Cook over a barbecue or under a preheated grill for 3–4 minutes on each side until cooked through, brushing with the ghee when the fish is turned. Serve garnished with a finely chopped small bunch of coriander.

 Spiced and Preserved Lemon Chargrilled Sardines Dry-fry 2 teaspoons each of cumin seeds and coriander seeds in a heavy-based frying pan over a medium heat for 1–2 minutes until they emit a nutty aroma. Tip them into a spice grinder and grind to a powder. Grate 1 onion into a bowl and add the powder with 1 teaspoon paprika, the finely chopped rind of 1 preserved lemon (see page 68) and a finely chopped small bunch of coriander. Mix with 3 tablespoons olive oil and season well. Rinse and pat dry 4–8 gutted sardines and, using a small, sharp knife, make several slashes along each side. Smear over the onion mixture, pressing it into the cuts. Leave to marinate for 10 minutes. Cook over a barbecue or under a preheated grill for 3–4 minutes on each side until cooked through, basting with any remaining marinade. Serve garnished with a finely chopped small bunch of coriander and the finely sliced rind of ½ preserved lemon.

MOR-GRIL-TAE

10 Seared Harissa Tuna Steaks

Serves 4

1 tablespoon olive oil, plus
extra for oiling

1 teaspoon harissa paste
(see page 70)

1 teaspoon runny honey

1 teaspoon sea salt

4 tuna steaks, about 150 g
(5 oz) each

small bunch of coriander,
finely chopped, to garnish

To serve

couscous

lemon wedges

- Mix together the oil, harissa, honey and salt in a small bowl, then rub over the tuna.

- Heat a lightly oiled large griddle pan or heavy-based frying pan until hot, add the tuna and sear for 2 minutes on each side until browned on the outside but still pink in the centre. Garnish with the coriander and serve with couscous, and lemon wedges to squeeze over.

 Harissa Tuna Steaks with Pan-Fried Almonds Melt 25 g (1 oz) butter in a frying pan, stir in 1–2 tablespoons flaked almonds and cook for 2–3 minutes until golden brown, then tip into a bowl. Rub the grated rind of 1 orange into the almonds. Mix together 1 tablespoon olive oil and 2 teaspoons harissa paste (see page 70) in a small bowl, then lightly brush over 4 tuna steaks. Heat an oiled griddle pan or frying pan, add the tuna and cook for 3–4 minutes on each side until browned on the outside but still pink in the middle. Season and serve with the almonds scattered over.

 Pan-Fried Tuna and Harissa Onions Heat 2 tablespoons olive or argan oil in a heavy-based frying pan, stir in 2 finely sliced onions, 2 finely chopped garlic cloves, 1 teaspoon coriander seeds and 2–3 bay leaves and cook for 1–2 minutes. Add the finely chopped rind of 1 fresh or preserved bitter orange, 1 teaspoon dried oregano and 1 teaspoon sugar, cover and cook over a medium heat for 5–6 minutes until the onions are softened. Remove the lid and continue to cook for 8–10 minutes until the onions are very soft and golden. Stir in 2 teaspoons harissa paste (see page 70), then add 4 tuna steaks, lifting the onion mixture over the top. Pour in about 75 ml (3 fl oz) white wine and cook for 6–8 minutes. Season well and serve garnished with a finely chopped small bunch of flat leaf parsley.

MOR-GRIL-QEY

 # Swordfish, Bay and Lime Kebabs

Serves 4

1 onion, grated

1–2 garlic cloves, crushed

2–3 teaspoons sumac

2 tablespoons olive oil

500 g (1 lb) skinless swordfish, boned and cut into bite-sized chunks

2 limes, cut into segments, plus extra to garnish

handful of fresh bay leaves

pepper

- Mix together the onion, garlic, most of the sumac and the oil in a shallow bowl. Season with pepper, then toss in the swordfish and leave to marinate for 10 minutes.

- Thread the fish onto 4 metal skewers, alternating with the lime segments and bay leaves. Cook over a barbecue or under a preheated grill for 2–3 minutes on each side until the swordfish is browned and cooked through. Sprinkle with the remaining sumac and serve immediately, with extra lime wedges to squeeze over.

 ### Swordfish, Bay and Tomato Kebabs

with Lime Thread 300 g (10 oz) skinless swordfish, boned and cut into bite-sized pieces, onto 4 metal skewers, alternating with 12 cherry tomatoes and a handful of fresh bay leaves. Brush with melted ghee or butter, then cook over a barbecue or under a preheated grill for 3 minutes on each side until the fish is cooked through, brushing with more melted ghee or butter. Sprinkle with 1–2 teaspoons sumac and serve with lime wedges.

 ### Swordfish, Scallop and Bay Kebabs

with Lime Place 12 scallops and 300 g (10 oz) skinless swordfish, boned and cut into bite-sized chunks, in a non-metallic bowl. Using a pestle and mortar, pound 2 chopped garlic cloves, 1 deseeded and chopped red chilli, 1 teaspoon cumin seeds, 1 teaspoon coriander seeds and 1 teaspoon sea salt to form a coarse paste. Whisk in 2 tablespoons olive oil and the juice of 2 limes. Pour the mixture over the swordfish and scallops and toss well. Cover and leave to marinate for 15 minutes. Thread the swordfish and scallops onto 4 metal skewers, adding a fresh bay leaf occasionally. Cook over a barbecue or under a preheated grill for 3–4 minutes on each side until cooked through, basting with any remaining marinade. Serve immediately with lime wedges to squeeze over.

30 Griddled Turmeric Squid with Crushed Chickpeas

Serves 4

2–4 fresh squid
juice of 1 lemon
3 tablespoons melted ghee,
  plus extra ghee for frying
1 onion, finely chopped
2 garlic cloves, finely chopped
1 red chilli, deseeded and
  finely chopped
1 teaspoon cumin seeds
400 g (13 oz) can chickpeas,
  rinsed and drained
2–3 teaspoons turmeric
salt and pepper
small bunch of flat leaf parsley,
  finely chopped, to garnish
lemon wedges, to serve

- To prepare the squid, hold the body in one hand and tug the head firmly with the other, so that the head and innards are released in one go. Remove the transparent backbone and rinse the body sac inside and out. Sever the tentacles just above the eyes and trim if long. Cut the squid sacs in half lengthways, score the inside with a knife in a diamond pattern, cut each half into 2 or 3 pieces and place in a non-metallic bowl with the lemon juice.

- Place 1 tablespoon of the ghee in a heavy-based frying pan, stir in the onion, garlic, chilli and cumin seeds and cook for 2–3 minutes. Stir in the chickpeas, mix well and season, then crush gently with a potato masher. Drizzle over 1 tablespoon of the ghee, cover with foil and keep warm.

- Pat the squid dry, then toss in the turmeric. Heat a griddle pan or heavy-based frying pan until hot and add a little ghee, then cook the squid in batches for 2–3 minutes until opaque and lightly browned. Season.

- Stir the remaining melted ghee into the crushed chickpeas and spoon onto a serving dish. Top with the squid, garnish with parsley and serve with lemon wedges to squeeze over.

---

10 Simple Pan-Fried Turmeric Squid

Slice about 250–300 g (8–10 oz) ready-prepared fresh squid into thin strips. Pat dry and toss with 2 teaspoons turmeric. Heat 1–2 tablespoons olive oil or ghee in a large, heavy-based frying pan, add the squid and cook for 3–4 minutes until opaque and lightly browned. Season and serve immediately with lime wedges to squeeze over.

20 Pan-Fried Spicy Turmeric Baby

Squid Prepare 8 baby squid by removing the head, innards and transparent backbone. Rinse the squid sacs, pat dry and sprinkle with 2 teaspoons turmeric. Heat 1 tablespoon olive oil or ghee in a large, heavy-based frying pan, stir in 2 finely chopped garlic cloves and 1 tablespoon peeled and finely chopped fresh root ginger and cook for 1–2 minutes until just beginning to colour. Add the squid and cook for 2–3 minutes on each side, or until opaque. Add 1 tablespoon honey, the juice of 1 lemon and 1–2 teaspoons harissa paste (see page 70) and cook gently for 4–5 minutes until beginning to caramelize. Season with salt, sprinkle with a little finely chopped coriander and serve immediately.

 # Chargrilled Chilli Prawns with Lime

Serves 4

2 tablespoons chilli oil
juice of 2 limes
2 tablespoons runny honey
½ teaspoon salt
12–16 raw prawns, shells on
lime wedges, to serve

- Put the chilli oil, lime juice, honey and salt in a non-metallic bowl and stir until the honey has dissolved. Slit the prawns along their backs and pull out the black vein, then toss in the marinade, pushing it into the shells. Leave to marinate for 10 minutes.

- Thread the prawns onto 4 metal skewers and cook over a barbecue or under a preheated grill for 2–3 minutes on each side until they turn pink and are cooked through. Serve immediately with lime wedges to squeeze over.

 Pan-Fried Chilli, Tabil and Lime Prawns Heat 2 tablespoons ghee or argan oil in a heavy-based frying pan, stir in 2–3 finely chopped garlic cloves and 1 deseeded and finely chopped red chilli and cook for 2–3 minutes. Add 2 teaspoons tabil spice mix and 450 g (14½ oz) raw peeled prawns, stir to coat well and cook for 4–5 minutes until they have turned pink and are cooked through. Stir in the juice of 1 lime and season. Serve with chunks of crusty bread and lime wedges to squeeze over.

Roasted Chilli and Lime Prawns and Carrots Put 500 g (1 lb) carrots, peeled and grated, 2 deseeded and finely sliced green chillies and 2 teaspoons cumin seeds in a roasting tin or ovenproof dish, then toss with 2–3 tablespoons olive oil. Place in a preheated oven, 180°C (350°F), Gas Mark 4, for 15–20 minutes. Place 12–16 large raw peeled prawns on the carrots and add the juice of 2 limes. Return to the oven and cook for a further 10 minutes, or until the prawns turn pink and are cooked through. Toss all the ingredients together with 1 tablespoon finely chopped coriander, season and serve with chunks of crusty bread.

MOR-GRIL-PUD

3◑ Mini Saffron Fish Balls

Serves 4

1 teaspoon saffron threads

450 g (14½ oz) skinless white fish
fillets, boned and finely flaked

1 onion, very finely chopped

1 red chilli, deseeded and very
finely chopped

finely chopped rind of 1 preserved
lemon (see page 68)

bunch of coriander, chopped

1 egg, beaten

sunflower oil, for frying

2 tablespoons dukkah spice mix
(for homemade, see page 118)

salt and pepper

lime wedges, to serve

- Using a pestle and mortar, grind the saffron to a powder and add a teaspoon of water. Place the fish in a bowl, add the saffron water and rub in well. Add the onion, chilli, preserved lemon rind and coriander and season. Mix well with a fork and stir in the egg. Knead the mixture until quite sticky, then roll into small balls.

- Heat enough oil in a large, heavy-based frying pan for shallow-frying, add the fish balls and cook, in batches, over a medium heat for 4–5 minutes until golden brown and cooked through. Drain on kitchen paper, then toss with the dukkah in a bowl. Serve with lime wedges to squeeze over.

 Fish Burgers with Saffron Butter

Place 225 g (7½ oz) drained canned tuna, 4 chopped spring onions, 2 teaspoons harissa paste (see page 70), 2–3 tablespoons fresh breadcrumbs and a chopped bunch of coriander in a bowl. Add 1 beaten egg and mix well. Knead well, then shape into 4 burgers. Heat enough sunflower oil for frying in a frying pan, add the burgers and cook for 3–4 minutes on each side. Meanwhile, melt 1–2 tablespoons butter in a saucepan, then stir in a pinch of saffron. Place the burgers on toasted flatbreads, pour over the saffron butter and serve with chopped onions, herbs and chutneys.

 Fishcakes with Saffron Lemon Juice Mix together the juice of 2 lemons and a pinch of saffron threads in a small bowl and set aside. Dry-fry 1–2 tablespoons sunflower seeds in a heavy-based frying pan over a medium heat for 2 minutes until they emit a nutty aroma. Put 225 g (7½ oz) drained canned tuna in a bowl with 1 finely chopped onion, 2 teaspoons harissa paste (see page 70), a finely chopped small bunch of flat leaf parsley and 1 beaten egg. Mix well with a fork, season and add 3–4 tablespoons fine fresh breadcrumbs. Knead the mixture, then roll into small balls. Flatten the balls in the palm of your hand, then lightly dip in plain flour. Heat enough sunflower oil for shallow-frying in a large, heavy-based frying pan, add the fishcakes and cook for 3–4 minutes on each side until golden brown and heated through. Transfer to a serving dish and spoon over the saffron lemon. Serve immediately with couscous.

30 Chermoula Fish and Vine Leaf Skewers

Serves 4

3–4 skinless white fish fillets, about 175 g (6 oz) each, such as haddock, or monkfish tails, boned

12–16 vine leaves in brine, drained and rinsed

For the chermoula

2–3 garlic cloves, chopped

1 red chilli, deseeded and chopped

1–2 teaspoons cumin seeds

1 teaspoon sea salt

small bunch of coriander, chopped

3–4 tablespoons olive oil

juice of 1 lemon

To serve (optional)

lemon wedges

harissa paste (see page 70)

- Make the chermoula. Using a pestle and mortar, pound the garlic, chilli, cumin seeds and salt to a coarse paste. Add the coriander and gradually whisk in the oil and lemon juice.

- Cut the fish fillets into 3–4 pieces each and place in a non-metallic bowl. Stir in the chermoula and leave to marinate for 10 minutes.

- Place the vine leaves on a flat surface and put a piece of marinated fish in the centre of each. Fold over the edges and wrap up into small parcels. Thread onto 4 large or 8 small metal skewers and brush with any remaining marinade.

- Cook the skewers over a barbecue or under a preheated grill for 3–4 minutes on each side until the fish is cooked through. Serve with lemon wedges to squeeze over and a dab of harissa paste, if liked.

---

10 Haloumi-Stuffed Vine Leaf Kebabs with Chermoula Dressing

In a bowl, toss together 225 g (7½ oz) haloumi cheese, cut into 8–10 bite-sized slices, 1–2 tablespoons olive oil and 1–2 teaspoons smoked paprika. Place 8–10 vine leaves in brine, drained and rinsed, on a flat surface, put a haloumi slice in the centre of each and fold over the edges to form tight parcels. Thread onto 4 large or 8 small metal skewers and cook over a barbecue or under a preheated grill for 2–3 minutes on each side. Mix together 2 tablespoons olive oil, the juice of 1 lemon and 1 tablespoon ready-made chermoula paste in a bowl. Serve the kebabs drizzled with the chermoula dressing.

20 Chermoula Scallop and Vine Leaf Kebabs

Place 12 scallops in a bowl, add 1 tablespoon olive or argan oil and 1 tablespoon ready-made chermoula paste and season. Toss and leave to marinate for 5 minutes. Place 12 vine leaves in brine, drained and rinsed, on a flat surface and put 1 marinated scallop in the centre of each. Fold over the edges to form small parcels, then thread onto 4 large or 8 small metal skewers. Cook over a barbecue or under a preheated grill for 3–4 minutes on each side. Serve with lemon wedges to squeeze over.

30 Vegetable Kebabs with Harissa Yogurt

Serves 4

1 aubergine, cut into chunks
2 courgettes, cut into chunks
2 peppers, deseeded and cubed
2 onions, cut into chunks
8–12 cherry tomatoes
2 tablespoons olive oil
juice of 1 lemon
2 garlic cloves, crushed
1 teaspoon ground coriander
1 teaspoon ground cinnamon
2 teaspoons runny honey
salt and pepper

For the yogurt

400 ml (14 fl oz) natural yogurt
2 garlic cloves, crushed
2–3 teaspoons harissa paste
  (see page 70)
small bunch of coriander, chopped
small bunch of mint, chopped

- Place all the vegetables and tomatoes in a non-metallic bowl. Mix together the oil, lemon juice, garlic, ground spices and honey in a small bowl, then season and pour over the vegetables. Toss well and leave to marinate for 5 minutes.

- To make the harissa yogurt, mix together the yogurt, garlic and harissa in a separate bowl, season and stir in the herbs, reserving some for garnish.

- Using your hands, toss the vegetables and tomatoes gently in the marinade, then thread alternately onto 8 metal skewers. Cook over a barbecue or under a preheated grill, brushing with any remaining marinade, for 3–4 minutes on each side until browned and tender. Sprinkle with the reserved herbs and serve immediately with the harissa yogurt.

 Tomato and Haloumi Kebabs with Harissa Oil Thread 225 g (7½ oz) haloumi, cut into chunks, and 12–16 cherry tomatoes onto metal skewers. Brush with 1 tablespoon melted ghee and cook over a barbecue or under a preheated grill for 2–3 minutes on each side, basting occasionally. Mix together 2–3 tablespoons olive or argan oil and 2 teaspoons harissa paste (see page 70) in a bowl. Season the kebabs, drizzle with the oil and serve immediately.

 Roasted Vegetables with Harissa Yogurt Scatter 2 diced aubergines, 2 diced courgettes, 1 cored, deseeded and diced red pepper and 1 diced onion in a roasting tin or ovenproof dish, add 3–4 smashed garlic cloves, 2 teaspoons coriander seeds and a few thyme sprigs and pour over 50 ml (2 fl oz) olive oil, the juice of 1 lemon and 1–2 teaspoons sugar. Season and toss well. Place in a preheated oven, 200°C (400°F), Gas Mark 6, for 25 minutes until the vegetables are tender and lightly browned. Meanwhile, make the Harissa Yogurt as above. Serve with the roasted vegetables.

MOR-GRIL-VYR

Pan-Fried Citrus Carrots and Mango

Serves 4-6

1–2 tablespoons olive or argan oil
1 onion, finely chopped
25 g (1 oz) fresh root ginger,
    peeled and finely chopped
2 garlic cloves, finely chopped
4–5 carrots, peeled and sliced
1 small, firm mango, peeled,
    stoned and thickly diced
1–2 teaspoons ras el hanout
juice of 2 limes
2 tablespoons orange
    blossom water
small bunch of flat leaf parsley,
    finely chopped
salt and pepper
lime wedges, to serve (optional)

- Heat the oil in a heavy-based frying pan, stir in the onion, ginger and garlic and cook for 2–3 minutes. Add the carrots and cook for 3–4 minutes until they begin to colour.

- Stir in the mango and ras el hanout. Add the lime juice and orange blossom water and cook gently for 4–5 minutes. Season, toss in half the parsley and garnish with the rest. Serve hot, with lime wedges to squeeze over, if liked.

Pan-Fried Spiced Dried Mango

Heat 1–2 tablespoons ghee in a heavy-based frying pan, stir in 1 teaspoon cumin seeds, 2 teaspoons coriander seeds and 2 crumbled bay leaves and cook for 1–2 minutes. Toss in 225 g (7½ oz) ready-to-eat dried mango, cut into thin strips, for 2–3 minutes and season with salt. Drain the mango on kitchen paper, then dust with 1 teaspoon ras el hanout. Serve hot.

Roasted Gingered Carrots and Mango

Scatter 4 peeled carrots, cut into matchsticks, and a thumb-sized piece of fresh root ginger, peeled and cut into thin matchsticks, in an ovenproof dish. Tuck in 4–6 fresh or dried bay leaves and pour over 2 tablespoons olive or argan oil. Place in a preheated oven, 200°C (400°F), Gas Mark 6, for 15 minutes. Mix in 1 firm mango, peeled, stoned and cut into matchsticks, season and drizzle over 1 tablespoon runny honey. Return to the oven and cook for a further 10 minutes. Serve with grilled or roasted meat and poultry.

Baby Aubergines with Honey and Harissa

Serves 4

8 baby aubergines, halved
   lengthways or thickly sliced
3 tablespoons olive oil
2–3 garlic cloves, finely chopped
25 g (1 oz) fresh root ginger,
   peeled and finely chopped
2 teaspoons cumin seeds
1–2 teaspoons harissa paste
   (see page 70)
4 tablespoons runny honey
juice of 1 lemon
200 ml (7 fl oz) water
salt and pepper
small bunch of coriander,
   finely chopped, to garnish
flatbread, to serve

- Brush the aubergines with some of the oil and cook them under a preheated medium-hot grill or in a griddle pan for 2–3 minutes on each side until lightly browned.

- Heat the remaining oil in a heavy-based frying pan, stir in the garlic, ginger and cumin seeds and cook for 2–3 minutes. Add the harissa, honey and lemon juice and pour in the measurement water. Stir well, then heat until bubbling and add the aubergines. Reduce the heat and cook gently for about 10 minutes until they have absorbed the sauce, adding more water if necessary. Season.

- Garnish with a little coriander and serve hot or at room temperature with flatbread.

 Deep-Fried Aubergines with Harissa Honey In a deep saucepan, heat enough sunflower oil for deep-frying to 180–190°C (350–375°F), or until a cube of bread browns in 30 seconds. Deep-fry the aubergine in the oil until golden brown. Melt 2 tablespoons honey in a small saucepan and stir in 1–2 teaspoons harissa paste (see page 70). Drain the aubergines on kitchen paper, then place on a serving dish and drizzle over the harissa honey. Garnish with a chopped small bunch of coriander and serve with grilled meats and poultry.

 Honey and Harissa Roasted Aubergines Cut 2 aubergines in half and, using a sharp knife, carefully remove and chop the flesh. Brush the inside of the empty aubergine shells with a little olive oil, put into an ovenproof dish and place in a preheated oven, 180°C (350°F), Gas Mark 4, for 4–5 minutes. Meanwhile, heat 2 tablespoons olive oil in a heavy-based frying pan, stir in 1 finely chopped onion and 2 finely chopped garlic cloves and cook for 1–2 minutes, then stir in the aubergine. Add a 400 g (13 oz) can tomatoes, drained of juice, 1 tablespoon honey, 2 teaspoons harissa paste (see page 70) and a finely chopped small bunch of coriander. Season well and stir in 2–3 tablespoons fresh breadcrumbs, then spoon into the roasted aubergine shells and top with 2 thinly sliced tomatoes. Dab each with a little butter and bake in the oven for 20 minutes. Serve hot, garnished with a finely chopped small bunch of coriander.

MOR-GRIL-KAO

30 Roasted Coriander and Preserved Lemon Potatoes

Serves 4

3 tablespoons ghee or butter

4 tablespoons finely chopped
coriander, plus extra to garnish

finely sliced rind of 1 preserved
lemon (see page 68)

1 kg (2¼ lb) potatoes, peeled and
finely sliced

salt and pepper

- Melt the ghee or butter in a small saucepan and stir in the coriander and preserved lemon rind. Place the potatoes in a large bowl and pour over the melted mixture and toss the potatoes well to coat.

- Spread the coated potatoes in an ovenproof dish, season and cover with foil. Place in a preheated oven, 200°C (400°F), Gas Mark 6, for 15 minutes. Remove the foil and return to the oven for a further 10 minutes until tender and lightly browned. Garnish with extra coriander and serve with roasted or grilled meat, poultry or fish.

1 Deep-Fried Coriander and Preserved Lemon Potatoes

In a deep saucepan, heat enough sunflower or vegetable oil for deep-frying to 180–190°C (350–375°F), or until a cube of bread browns in 30 seconds. Deep-fry 700 g (1½ lb) new potatoes, peeled and finely sliced, in batches until golden brown. Mix together 1 tablespoon finely chopped coriander and the finely chopped rind of 1 preserved lemon (see page 68). Drain the potatoes on kitchen paper, then place on a serving dish and scatter over the coriander and preserved lemon.

2 Spicy Coriander and Preserved Lemon Potatoes

Cook 700 g (1½ lb) peeled new potatoes in a saucepan of boiling water for 7–10 minutes, or until just cooked. Drain and refresh under cold running water, then chop into bite-sized pieces. Heat 2 tablespoons ghee in a large, heavy-based frying pan, add 3–4 finely chopped garlic cloves, 1–2 deseeded and finely chopped red or green chillies, 2 teaspoons cumin seeds and 1 teaspoon coriander seeds and cook for 2 minutes. Stir in 2 teaspoons turmeric, then add the potatoes and cook for 1–2 minutes, stirring to coat well. Add the juice of 1 lemon, 1 tablespoon finely chopped coriander and the finely chopped rind of 1 preserved lemon (see page 68). Cook gently for 3–4 minutes until the potatoes have absorbed the flavours, then season. Garnish with a finely chopped small bunch of coriander and serve with grilled and roasted meat, poultry or fish.

30 Roasted Spiced Pumpkin

Serves 4

2 teaspoons coriander seeds

2 teaspoons cumin seeds

2–3 garlic cloves

1–2 teaspoons sea salt

1 teaspoon finely chopped dried
red chilli or cayenne powder

1 teaspoon ground cinnamon

1 teaspoon ground allspice

3 tablespoons olive or argan oil

1 small pumpkin, halved, deseeded
and cut into thin wedges

- Using a pestle and mortar, pound the coriander and cumin seeds, garlic and salt to form a coarse paste. Stir in the chilli or cayenne, cinnamon and allspice, then mix in the oil.

- Rub the mixture over the pumpkin wedges, then place, skin side down, in a roasting tin or ovenproof dish. Roast in a preheated oven, 200°C (400°F), Gas Mark 6, for 25 minutes until tender. Serve with grilled or roasted meat dishes.

Roasted Pumpkin Seeds

Heat 1 tablespoon sunflower or argan oil in a small, heavy-based frying pan, stir in about 225 g (7½ oz) dried pumpkin seeds, still in their shells with the fibres rubbed off. Toss over a high heat for 3–4 minutes, then stir in 1 tablespoon ghee or butter and cook for a further 3–4 minutes until lightly browned. Toss in 1 teaspoon sea salt, then drain the seeds on kitchen paper. To eat, gently crack open the seed with your teeth, extract the kernel and discard the shell.

Pan-Fried Spicy Pumpkin

Heat 2 tablespoons ghee or argan oil in a heavy-based frying pan, stir in 1 teaspoon each of fennel seeds and coriander seeds and cook for 1–2 minutes. Add 50 g (2 oz) fresh root ginger, peeled and finely chopped, and 1 deseeded and finely chopped red chilli and cook for a further 1–2 minutes. Add 700 g (1½ lb) peeled, deseeded and diced pumpkin and toss well to coat, then pour in 100 ml (3½ fl oz) water, or enough to just cover the base of the pan. Cover and cook gently for 10 minutes until the pumpkin is tender and the pan is almost dry. Drizzle in 1–2 tablespoons runny honey, season, toss well and cook gently for 4–5 minutes. Serve hot as a side dish, garnished with a finely chopped small bunch of coriander.

1 Deep-Fried Plantain Chips with Zahtar

Serves 4

2 large, ripe plantains
sunflower oil, for deep-frying
coarse sea salt
1–2 tablespoons zahtar

- In a deep saucepan, heat enough oil for deep-frying to 180–190°C (350–375°F), or until a cube of bread browns in 30 seconds.

- Meanwhile, to peel the plantains, use a sharp knife to chop off the ends, then slit the skins lengthways and remove the peel in strips. Slice the plantains quite finely.

- Deep-fry the plantain in the oil in batches for 2–3 minutes until golden brown. Remove with a slotted spoon and drain on kitchen paper, then sprinkle well with sea salt. Tip the slices into a bowl, toss with the zahtar and serve immediately.

2 Deep-Fried Baby Plantains with Chermoula

Using a pestle and mortar, pound 2 deseeded and chopped red chillies, 2 chopped garlic cloves and a little sea salt to form a coarse paste. Mix in 2–3 tablespoons olive oil, the juice of 1 lemon, 1–2 teaspoons runny honey and 1 tablespoon finely chopped coriander. Peel 2–3 baby plantains as above, then cut in half lengthways. In a deep saucepan, heat enough sunflower oil for deep-frying to 180–190°C (350–375°F), or until a cube of bread browns in 30 seconds. Deep-fry the plantains for 6–8 minutes until just golden brown. Remove with a slotted spoon and drain on kitchen paper. Transfer to a plate and drizzle over the sauce.

3 Roasted Spicy Baby Plantains

Peel 4 baby plantains as above, then put into a saucepan, cover with water and bring to the boil. Add 1 teaspoon salt and boil for 6–8 minutes. Drain and refresh under cold running water, then place in an ovenproof dish with 3–4 cinnamon sticks and 2–3 dried red chillies. Pour over 2 tablespoons melted butter, sprinkle with 1–2 teaspoons finely chopped dried red chilli and drizzle with 1–2 tablespoons runny honey. Place in a preheated oven, 180°C (350°F), Gas Mark 4, for 15–20 minutes until slightly caramelized. Serve with grilled or roasted poultry.

MOR-GRIL-JYT

QuickCook

Sweet Snacks, Desserts and Drinks

Recipes listed by cooking time

3

2

10

Watermelon, Rosewater and Lemon Balm Salad

Serves 4

½ ripe watermelon or 1 large wedge, about 900 g (2 lb) total weight
2–3 tablespoons rosewater
1 tablespoon lemon balm or mint leaves, finely shredded, plus extra to decorate
icing sugar, for dusting

- Remove the skin and seeds from the watermelon. Place the flesh on a plate to catch the juice and cut into bite-sized cubes. Tip the cubes into a shallow freezer-proof bowl and pour over the juice. Add the rosewater and the shredded mint or lemon balm and toss gently.

- Chill in the freezer for at least 5 minutes. Just before serving, dust with icing sugar and decorate with extra mint or lemon balm leaves.

2 — Watermelon, Pomegranate and Rosewater Salad

Deseed and dice 250 g (8 oz) watermelon flesh and put into a freezer-proof bowl. Cut 2 ripe pomegranates into quarters then, holding them over the watermelon bowl to catch the juice, bend each quarter backwards and flick the seeds into the bowl, leaving behind the white membrane and pith. Gently stir in 2–3 tablespoons rosewater and 1–2 teaspoons granulated sugar, then chill in the freezer for 10 minutes before serving.

3 — Watermelon and Rose Petal Conserve with Yogurt

Place 450 g (14½ oz) granulated sugar and 125 ml (4 fl oz) water in a heavy-based saucepan and slowly bring to the boil, stirring continuously until the sugar has dissolved. Add the rind, cut into thin strips, and juice of 1 lemon, 2 tablespoons rosewater and 250 g (8 oz) deseeded and diced watermelon flesh. Bring to the boil, then reduce the heat and simmer gently for 15 minutes. Stir in 2 tablespoons fresh scented rose petals and cook gently for a further 8–10 minutes.

Serve with thick strained yogurt. (The cooled conserve can also be stored in sealed sterilized jars for several months.)

Orange Blossom and Cinnamon Orange Salad

Serves 4

5–6 ripe oranges

2 tablespoons orange
blossom water

2 teaspoons icing sugar

1 teaspoon ground cinnamon

- Using a sharp knife, remove the peel and pith from the oranges. Place the oranges on a plate to catch the juice and thinly slice, removing any seeds. Arrange the orange slices in a serving dish.

- Tip the orange juice into a bowl and stir in the orange blossom water. Pour the juice over the oranges, dust with icing sugar and sprinkle over the cinnamon. Serve immediately.

 Oranges with Orange Blossom and Cinnamon Syrup Place the grated rind of 2 oranges, 300 ml (½ pint) water, 200 g (7 oz) granulated sugar and 2 cinnamon sticks in a small saucepan and bring to the boil, then boil for 2–3 minutes, stirring continuously until the sugar has dissolved. Stir in 2 tablespoons orange blossom water, reduce the heat and cook gently for 10 minutes. Meanwhile, using a sharp knife, remove the peel and pith from the grated oranges and an extra 2–3 oranges, then thinly slice, removing the seeds. Cut the slices into quarters and put into a bowl. Pour over the hot syrup and leave to cool.

 Baked Cinnamon Oranges Using a sharp knife, cut 2 ripe oranges in half horizontally, then separate the segments from the pith and remove the seeds. Place the 4 orange halves, cut side up, in an ovenproof dish. Mix together 1 tablespoon granulated sugar and 2 teaspoons ground cinnamon in a bowl, then scatter over the oranges. Dot each one with a knob of butter and place in a preheated oven, 180°C (350°F), Gas Mark 4, for 20–25 minutes. Dust with icing sugar and serve hot with cream, yogurt or ice cream.

Spiced Quince Jam

Serves 4

450 g (14½ oz) fresh quinces
squeeze of lemon juice
350 g (11½ oz) granulated sugar
225 ml (7½ fl oz) water
2 cinnamon sticks
1 vanilla pod
2–3 star anise
6 cloves
2 strips of lemon rind
mini pancakes, to serve

- Peel and core each quince, then place in a bowl of water with the lemon juice to prevent discoloration.

- Place the sugar and measurement water in a heavy-based saucepan and bring to the boil, stirring continuously until the sugar has dissolved. Add the spices and lemon rind, then reduce the heat and simmer gently for 2–3 minutes.

- Meanwhile, coarsely grate the quinces, then add to the syrup and simmer gently for a further 15–20 minutes. Serve the hot jam spooned over mini pancakes. (The cooled jam can also be stored in sealed sterilized jars for 2–3 months.)

 Quinces with Clove Icing Sugar

Quarter and core 2 quinces, then finely slice each quarter. Place in a bowl and squeeze over the juice of 1 lemon. Sift 2–3 tablespoons icing sugar and ½ teaspoon ground cloves into a small serving dish and serve with the quinces. To eat, dip the slices of quince into the sugar.

 Poached Quinces in Clove Syrup

Place 300 ml (½ pint) water and 175 g (6 oz) granulated sugar in a heavy-based saucepan and bring to the boil, stirring continuously until the sugar has dissolved. Stir in the juice of ½ lemon, 2 tablespoons rosewater and 4–5 cloves and cook gently for 5 minutes to form a light syrup. Meanwhile, peel, core and deseed 2 large quinces, then cut into 6–8 thick segments and place in a bowl of water with a squeeze of lemon juice. Drain the quince segments, add them to the syrup and poach gently for 15 minutes. Leave to cool slightly in the pan, then serve with clotted cream, strained yogurt or ice cream.

 Date and Pistachio Truffles

Serves 4

225 g (7½ oz) shelled pistachio nuts
225 g (7½ oz) ready-to-eat pitted dates, chopped
1 tablespoon orange blossom water
1 teaspoon ground cinnamon
1 tablespoon runny honey
50 g (2 oz) desiccated coconut

• Dry-fry the pistachios in a heavy-based frying pan over a medium heat for 1–2 minutes until they begin to colour and emit a nutty aroma. Put into a food processor with the dates and blend to a thick paste.

• Transfer the paste to a bowl and knead in the orange blossom water, cinnamon and honey. Roll about 16 small pieces of the mixture into bite-sized balls.

• Sprinkle the coconut onto a plate. Roll the truffles in the coconut until evenly coated. Serve with coffee or tea.

Stuffed Almond Dates

Mix together 150 g (5 oz) ground almonds, 60 g (2¼ oz) caster sugar and 1 tablespoon rosewater in a bowl, then work to a smooth, soft paste, adding more rosewater if needed. Place 200 g (7 oz) ready-to-eat pitted dates on a plate and stuff each one with the almond paste. Press the stuffed dates gently to compress the filling, leaving them slightly open to reveal the paste. Serve with coffee or tea.

Mini Pistachio and Date Pastries

Place 225 g (7½ oz) ready-to-eat pitted dates, 120 g (4 oz) shelled pistachio nuts and 1 teaspoon orange rind in a food processor and blend to a thick paste. Sift 225 g (7½ oz) plain flour into a bowl then, using your fingertips, rub in 120 g (4 oz) butter, cut into small pieces. Add 1–2 tablespoons orange blossom water and work to a smooth, soft dough. Roll about 20 small pieces of the dough into balls. Hollow out each ball with

your finger and pinch the sides to form a tiny pot. Fill each about three-quarters full with the date paste and pull over the dough to enclose the filling. Slightly flatten the balls, make a small dent on the tops with the back of a fork and place on a lightly oiled baking sheet. Bake in a preheated oven, 200°C (400°F), Gas Mark 6, for 10–12 minutes until lightly golden. Leave to cool and firm up, then dust with icing sugar and serve with coffee or tea.

30 Sweet Cinnamon, Pistachio and Raisin Couscous

Serves 4

250 g (8 oz) fine couscous

2 teaspoons ground cinnamon, plus extra for dusting

½ teaspoon ground cloves

1–2 tablespoons granulated sugar

300 ml (½ pint) boiling water

1 tablespoon sunflower oil

60 g (2¼ oz) butter

120 g (4 oz) shelled unsalted pistachio nuts

2–3 tablespoons sultanas or raisins

125 ml (4 fl oz) milk

125 ml (4 fl oz) double cream

4 tablespoons runny honey

- Put the couscous into a heatproof bowl and stir in the cinnamon, cloves and sugar. Pour over the boiling measurement water, cover and leave to stand for 10–15 minutes. Drizzle the oil over the couscous and, using your fingertips, rub it into separate the grains.

- Melt the butter in a heavy-based frying pan, stir in the pistachios and cook until they emit a nutty aroma. Add the sultanas or raisins and cook until plump, then tip the mixture over the couscous. Toss well and spoon the couscous into 4 serving bowls.

- Meanwhile, heat the milk and cream in a small saucepan. Pour over the couscous and drizzle over the honey. Serve immediately, with a dusting of cinnamon.

 Sweet Cinnamon Couscous Balls

Tip 350 g (11½ oz) couscous into a heatproof bowl and just cover with boiling water. Cover with clingfilm and leave to stand for 5 minutes, then fluff up with a fork. Leave to cool slightly then, using your fingers, rub the grains to loosen and mould small pieces into balls, squeezing them together. Roll the balls in 2 tablespoons icing sugar and dust with 1 teaspoon ground cinnamon.

 Sweet Cinnamon Couscous Pudding

Put 300 g (10 oz) couscous in a heatproof bowl and stir in 350 ml (12 fl oz) warm water. Cover and leave to stand for 10 minutes. Fluff up the couscous with a fork, then rub the grains between your fingers to separate them. Bring 300 ml (½ pint) milk to just below boiling point, then stir in 2–3 tablespoons muscovado or soft brown sugar until it has dissolved. Stir in the couscous and cook gently for 4–5 minutes. Dust the top with ground cinnamon and serve immediately for breakfast or as a snack.

MOR-SWEE-MOJ

30 Orange and Honey Puffs in Citrus Syrup

Serves 4

3 eggs
juice of 1 orange
grated rind of 2 oranges,
  plus extra to garnish
50 ml (2 fl oz) sunflower oil,
  plus extra for deep-frying
2 tablespoons runny honey
350 g (11½ oz) plain flour,
  plus extra for dusting
1 teaspoon baking powder

For the syrup

225 g (7½ oz) granulated sugar
250 ml (8 fl oz) water
juice of 1 lemon
1–2 tablespoons orange
  blossom water

- In a bowl, whisk together the eggs, orange juice, orange rind and oil until frothy, then stir in the honey. Sift in 300 g (10 oz) of the flour and the baking powder and beat to form a thick batter.

- To make the syrup, place the sugar and measurement water in a heavy-based saucepan and bring to the boil, stirring until the sugar has dissolved. Stir in the lemon juice, reduce the heat and simmer for 10 minutes until syrupy. Stir in the orange blossom water and simmer over a low heat.

- Beat the remaining flour into the batter until it forms a pliable dough. Tip onto a lightly floured surface and roll out to about 5 mm (¼ inch) thick, pulling out the dough until it stops springing back. Using a 5–7 cm (2–3 inch) cutter, cut out about 16 rounds.

- In a saucepan, heat enough oil for deep-frying to 180–190°C (350–375°F), or until a cube of bread browns in 30 seconds. Deep-fry the dough in batches for 2–3 minutes until puffed up and golden brown. Remove with a slotted spoon and drain on kitchen paper. Using tongs, dip the puffs into the syrup and serve immediately, garnished with grated orange rind.

 Ice Cream with Orange and Honey Sauce Put 125 ml (4 fl oz) water into a small saucepan and stir in 1 teaspoon cornflour until it has dissolved. Add the grated rind and juice of 1 orange, 2–3 tablespoons orange blossom water and 2 tablespoons honey, then bring to the boil over a medium heat. Reduce the heat and simmer for 3–4 minutes. Serve spooned over vanilla ice cream.

 Orange and Honey Puffs in Cinnamon Sugar Make the Orange and Honey Puffs as above. In a large bowl, mix together 3 tablespoons granulated sugar and 2 teaspoons ground cinnamon. Tip the drained puffs into the bowl, cover with a plate or lid and shake well to coat. Serve the puffs with coffee or tea.

20 Pistachio, Lime and Coconut Cakes

Serves 4

225 g (7½ oz) shelled unsalted pistachio nuts

50 g (2 oz) desiccated coconut

200 g (7 oz) soft brown sugar

grated rind and juice of 1 lime

2 eggs

2 egg yolks

icing sugar, for dusting

- Place 12 paper cake cases on a baking sheet. Put the pistachios and coconut in a food processor and whizz until ground. Add the brown sugar, lime rind and juice and blend to a paste. Add the eggs and egg yolks and blend until smooth.

- Drop 1 heaped tablespoon of the mixture into each cake case. Bake in a preheated oven, 200°C (400°F), Gas Mark 6, for 12–15 minutes until slightly firm to the touch.

- Leave the cakes to cool slightly, then dust with icing sugar and serve with coffee or tea.

 1 Pistachio, Lime and Coconut Topped Ice Cream Dry-fry 250 g (8 oz) shelled unsalted pistachio nuts in a heavy-based frying pan over a medium heat for 1–2 minutes until they emit a nutty aroma. Toss in 2–3 tablespoons desiccated coconut and the grated rind of 1 lime and toast for 1 minute, then stir in 1 tablespoon ghee or butter until it melts. Add 1 tablespoon granulated sugar and stir continuously until it has dissolved. Serve hot over vanilla ice cream.

 3 Coconut and Lime Biscuits In a bowl, cream together 100 g (3½ oz) softened butter and 100 g (3½ oz) granulated sugar for 3–4 minutes until light and fluffy. Beat in 50 g (2 oz) desiccated coconut, the grated rind of 1 lime and 1 teaspoon lime juice, then beat in 1 egg. Sift in 175 g (6 oz) plain flour, 1 teaspoon cream of tartar, ½ teaspoon bicarbonate of soda and a pinch of salt and, using your fingers, work to form a dough. Knead until smooth, then place on a piece of greaseproof paper and roll into a cylinder about 5 cm (2 inches) in diameter. Tuck the paper around the dough and place in the freezer for 10–15 minutes. Cut the dough into thin slices and place on a lightly oiled baking sheet. Bake in a preheated oven, 200°C (400°F), Gas Mark 6, for 6–7 minutes. Transfer to a wire rack and leave to cool.

MOR-SWEE-GYH

30 Baked Honey, Cardamom and Cinnamon Figs

Serves 4

12 ripe fresh figs
1 tablespoon ghee or butter,
   plus extra for greasing
2 teaspoons cardamom seeds
2 cinnamon sticks
grated rind of 1 lemon
4–5 tablespoons honey
strained yogurt, crème fraîche
   or clotted cream, to serve
icing sugar, for dusting

- Cut each fig lengthways into quarters, keeping the base intact, and place in a lightly greased ovenproof dish.

- Melt the ghee or butter in a small saucepan, stir in the cardamom seeds, cinnamon sticks, lemon rind and honey and cook for 2 minutes until bubbling. Pour the mixture evenly over the figs.

- Bake in a preheated oven, 200°C (400°F), Gas Mark 6, for 20 minutes. Serve dusted with icing sugar accompanied by yogurt, crème fraîche or clotted cream, to be dolloped into the middle of each fig.

 Creamy Figs with Cinnamon Honey

Place 8 ripe fresh figs on a plate and, using a small, sharp knife, cut a deep cross into the top of each one, keeping the base intact. Put a spoonful of clotted cream or strained yogurt into the hollow and drizzle each one with 1 tablespoon runny honey. Dust with ground cinnamon and serve.

 Pancakes with Dried Fig, Cinnamon and Aniseed Jam

Put 300 ml (½ pint) water and 225 g (7½ oz) granulated sugar into a heavy-based saucepan and bring to the boil, stirring continuously until the sugar has dissolved. Reduce the heat and simmer for 5 minutes until the syrup begins to thicken. Stir in the juice of 1 lemon, 1 teaspoon ground cinnamon, 1 teaspoon ground aniseed and 350 g (11½ oz) roughly chopped ready-to-eat dried figs. Bring to the boil, then reduce the heat and simmer for 12 minutes until the figs are tender. Meanwhile, heat 4 ready-made pancakes according to the packet instructions. Serve with the hot jam and clotted cream or strained yogurt. (The cooled jam can also be stored in sealed sterilized jars for 2–3 months.)

30 Spicy Nut and Raisin Truffles

Serves 4

450 g (14½ oz) blanched almonds
200 g (7 oz) walnuts
450 g (14½ oz) raisins
120 g (4 oz) butter
200 g (7 oz) honey
1 teaspoon ras el hanout
1 teaspoon ground cinnamon
½ teaspoon ground ginger
4 tablespoons sesame seeds

- Using a pestle and mortar or a food processor, pound or blend the nuts and raisins to a coarse paste.

- Melt the butter in a heavy-based saucepan, stir in the honey and spices, then add the paste. Stir over a low heat until the mixture reaches a jam-like consistency. Turn off the heat and leave to cool.

- Using wet fingertips, roll about 25 small pieces of the mixture into truffle-sized balls. Place the sesame seeds on a plate. Roll the truffles in the seeds until evenly coated and serve.

 Spicy Almond and Raisin Honey Yogurt Melt 300 g (10 oz) runny honey in a small saucepan. Stir in 2 tablespoons raisins, 2 tablespoons halved blanched almonds and ½ teaspoon ras el hanout. Bring to the boil, then remove from the heat, stir and leave to cool slightly to let the flavours mingle. Spoon 2–3 tablespoons thick natural yogurt into each of 4 bowls and spoon over the honey.

 Baked Spicy Almond and Raisin Balls Place 200 g (7 oz) ground almonds, 150 g (5 oz) granulated sugar and the grated rind of 1 lemon in a food processor and blend with 2 tablespoons water. Add 1 teaspoon ground cinnamon and ½ teaspoon ras el hanout and blend again until the mixture forms a soft paste. Roll about 20 small pieces of the mixture into balls. Make a hollow in each with your finger, fill each with a plump raisin and close up to seal. Place the balls on a baking sheet lined with greaseproof paper and bake in a preheated oven, 200°C (400°F), Gas Mark 6, for 6–8 minutes until lightly golden. Lightly dust with icing sugar and leave to cool slightly before serving.

MOR-SWEE-SIQ

 Hot Spiced Dried Fruit Compote

Serves 4

225 g (7½ oz) granulated or
  soft brown sugar
1 litre (1¾ pints) water
2 cinnamon sticks
4–6 cloves
2 star anise
juice of 1 lime
100 g (3½ oz) ready-to-eat
  pitted dried prunes
100 g (3½ oz) ready-to-eat
  dried apricots
100 g (3½ oz) ready-to-eat
  dried figs
90 g (3¼ oz) blanched almonds
1 tablespoon sesame seeds
icing sugar, for dusting
natural yogurt or cream,
  to serve

- Put the sugar and measurement water into a heavy-based saucepan and bring to the boil, stirring continuously until the sugar has dissolved. Stir in the spices, reduce the heat and simmer for 10 minutes. Stir in the lime juice, dried fruit and almonds and cook gently for a further 8 minutes.

- Meanwhile, in a small, heavy-based frying pan, dry-fry the sesame seeds over a medium heat for 1–2 minutes until they emit a nutty aroma.

- Scatter the compote with the toasted seeds and dust with icing sugar. Serve with yogurt or cream.

Quick Dried Fruit Compote

Place 250 g (8 oz) ready-to-eat dried apricots, 250 g (8 oz) ready-to-eat pitted dried prunes, 150 g (5 oz) sultanas and 150 g (5 oz) blanched almonds in a bowl. Pour over enough water to just cover the fruit, then add 175 g (6 oz) granulated sugar and 2–3 tablespoons orange blossom water and stir gently until the sugar has dissolved. Serve for breakfast or as a snack with couscous or pancakes.

Spiced Dried Fruit and Wine Compote

Place 225 g (7½ oz) ready-to-eat dried figs, halved, 225 g (7½ oz) ready-to-eat dried apricots and 225 g (7½ oz) ready-to-eat pitted dried prunes in an ovenproof dish. Add 2–3 cinnamon sticks, 4–6 cloves and 2 dried bay leaves. Pour in 300 ml (½ pint) white wine and sprinkle over 1 tablespoon soft brown or muscovado sugar. Bake in a preheated oven, 180°C (350°F), Gas Mark 4, for 15 minutes.

Toss the fruit well and sprinkle with 1 tablespoon soft brown or muscovado sugar, then return to the oven for a further 10 minutes. Serve hot with strained yogurt, clotted cream or ice cream.

 Simple Fresh Fruit Kebabs

Serves 4

4 fresh apricots, halved
   and stoned
4 fresh figs, quartered
½ galia melon, peeled,
   deseeded and cubed
thick wedge of watermelon,
   peeled, deseeded and cubed
small bunch of mint leaves
2 limes, quartered
icing sugar, for dusting

- Thread the fruit onto 8 metal skewers, sticks or twigs, alternating with the mint leaves and finishing with the lime quarters.

- Dust the fruit with icing sugar and serve, squeezing the lime over the fruit before eating.

 Chilled Rosewater Fruit Salad

Peel, deseed and chop ½ galia melon and place in a freezer-proof bowl. Add 2 halved, stoned and chopped peaches, 2 peeled, cored and chopped pears, 2 sliced bananas and the juice of 1 lemon and mix well. Add 225 g (7½ oz) halved and stoned cherries, 225 g (7½ oz) green grapes and 3–4 tablespoons fresh pomegranate seeds. Stir in 3–4 tablespoons rosewater, then chill in the freezer for 10 minutes. Dust with icing sugar and serve.

Poached Red Wine and Rosewater Fruit Peel, quarter and core 2 apples and 3 pears. Slice each quarter in half and place in a bowl with a squeeze of lemon juice to prevent discoloration. Bring 500 ml (17 fl oz) red wine, 100 g (3½ oz) granulated sugar, 2 cinnamon sticks and the rind of 1 lemon, cut into strips, to the boil in a heavy-based saucepan, stirring continuously until the sugar has dissolved. Add the apples and pears and bring to the boil, then reduce the heat and cook gently for 12–15 minutes until just tender. Add 8 halved, stoned and quartered apricots and 4 tablespoons rosewater and cook gently for a further 8–10 minutes until tender but still retaining a little bite. Dust with icing sugar and serve hot with dollops of clotted cream, strained yogurt or ice cream.

MOR-SWEE-FAN

30 Baked Almond and Orange Blossom Apricots

Serves 4

12 fresh apricots
200 g (7 oz) blanched almonds
120 g (4 oz) caster sugar
3 tablespoons orange
  blossom water
1–2 tablespoons runny honey

- Using a sharp knife, slit open the apricots down one side and remove the stones.

- Place the almonds, sugar and orange blossom water in a food processor and blend to a soft paste. Roll 12 small pieces of the paste into balls, then stuff into the apricots. Press the apricots gently to compress the filling and place in an ovenproof dish.

- Bake in a preheated oven, 180°C (350°F), Gas Mark 4, for 15 minutes. Drizzle over the honey, then return to the oven and cook for a further 5–6 minutes. Serve hot or cold.

 1 Nut and Orange Blossom Dried Apricots Drain 450 g (14½ oz) ready-to-eat dried apricots, soaked overnight in 1 litre (1¾ pints) water, and reserve the soaking liquid. Put one-third of the apricots into a food processor and blend to a purée with the soaking water. Add 2 tablespoons granulated sugar and 3 tablespoons orange blossom water, then pour over the remaining apricots in a bowl. Stir in 2 tablespoons roughly chopped blanched almonds and 2 tablespoons roughly chopped shelled pistachio nuts. Serve with ice cream or strained yogurt.

 2 Poached Orange Blossom and Almond Apricots Drain 250 g (8 oz) ready-to-eat dried apricots, soaked in 600 ml (1 pint) water overnight, and put the soaking liquid into a saucepan with 225 g (7½ oz) granulated sugar. Bring to the boil, stirring continuously until the sugar has dissolved, then boil gently for a further 4–5 minutes. Stir in 2–3 tablespoons orange blossom water, the drained apricots and 2 tablespoons blanched almonds. Bring to the boil, then reduce the heat and cook gently for 12–15 minutes. Serve hot with pancakes and ice cream.

30 Thick Semolina Pancakes with Honey

Serves 4

225 g (7½ oz) plain flour, plus extra for dusting
½ teaspoon salt
225 g (7½ oz) fine semolina
300 ml (½ pint) warm water
3 tablespoons melted ghee
4–5 tablespoons runny honey

- Sift the flour and salt into a bowl and stir in the semolina. Gradually pour in the measurement water and mix to form a soft dough. Knead well for about 5 minutes until smooth and pliable. Divide into 8 pieces and roll into ping pong-sized balls. Place on a lightly floured surface, cover with a clean, damp tea towel and leave to rest for 10 minutes.

- Flatten and stretch each ball into a thin disc about 18 cm (7 inches) in diameter. Brush with melted ghee and fold a third of it into the middle, the next third overlapping it, and the final third on top, so that you end up with a square parcel. Flatten each parcel and roll or stretch to about 15 cm (6 inches) square.

- Heat a heavy-based griddle pan and brush with a little of the melted ghee. Add the pancakes in batches and cook, brushing with melted ghee, for about 2 minutes on each side until browned.

- Heat the honey in a small saucepan and drizzle over the pancakes. Serve for breakfast or as a hot snack.

 Quick Pancakes with Honey

Heat 4 ready-made pancakes according to the packet instructions. Meanwhile, heat 4 tablespoons honey in a small saucepan. Place the pancakes on 4 serving plates, drizzle with the honey and roll up. Drizzle over more honey and serve immediately with a sprinkling of roasted chopped nuts or toasted coconut.

 Toasted Coconut and Honey Pancake Stacks Sift 120 g (4 oz) plain flour and a pinch of salt into a bowl, make a well in the centre and pour in 1 beaten egg. Gradually add 300 ml (½ pint) milk and beat to a smooth batter. Beat in 1 teaspoon sunflower oil and set aside. Dry-fry 4 tablespoons desiccated coconut in a saucepan over a medium heat for 2–3 minutes until lightly browned and it emits a nutty aroma. Heat a nonstick pancake pan, wipe it with a little sunflower oil and add a ladleful of the batter, swirling it around to form a thin layer. Cook for 1–2 minutes on each side until golden brown. Tip onto a plate and keep warm. Repeat with the remaining batter, adding a little more oil if necessary. Heat 4–5 tablespoons honey in a small saucepan and layer up the pancakes, sprinkling with the toasted coconut and drizzling a little honey over each one. Divide the stack into 4. Top with the remaining honey and toasted coconut and serve immediately.

Crystallized Rose Petals

Serves 4

2 egg whites
2–3 tablespoons caster sugar
2 sweet-scented, opened roses

- Line a baking sheet with greaseproof paper. In a spotlessly clean bowl, whisk the egg whites with a hand-held electric whisk until stiff.

- Tip the sugar onto a plate. Carefully pull the rose petals off the flower heads. Brush a rose petal with a little egg white, then dip into the sugar. Shake off any excess and place on the greaseproof paper to dry. Repeat with the remaining rose petals.

- For best results, leave for 1–2 hours until completely dry. Peel off the paper, then use to decorate puddings, cakes and milk drinks.

Rose Syrup Cordial

Place 450 g (14½ oz) granulated sugar and 225 ml (7½ fl oz) water in a heavy-based saucepan and bring to the boil, stirring continuously until the sugar has dissolved. Add the juice of ½ lemon and simmer for 5 minutes. Stir in 100 ml (3½ fl oz) rosewater and simmer for 4–5 minutes. Leave to cool in the pan, then pass through a sieve into a sterilized bottle or jar. To serve, put a few ice cubes into a glass, add 2–3 tablespoons rose syrup and top up with cold water. (The cordial can also be stored in the refrigerator for 3–4 weeks.)

Rosewater Milk Pudding

In a small bowl, mix together 2 heaped tablespoons rice flour and 75 ml (3 fl oz) milk to form a loose paste. Set aside. Place 700 ml (1¼ pints) milk and 125 g (4 oz) granulated sugar in a heavy-based saucepan and bring to the boil, stirring continuously until the sugar has dissolved. Reduce the heat and stir 1–2 spoonfuls of the hot milk into the rice flour paste, then tip the mixture into the pan, stirring continuously to prevent any lumps forming. Return to boiling point, then stir in 2–3 tablespoons rosewater, reduce the heat to low and simmer gently for 20 minutes, stirring occasionally, until thickened. Serve hot with a dusting of icing sugar.

MOR-SWEE-PEH

30 Almond and Cinnamon Filo Coil

Serves 4

450 g (14½ oz) ground almonds
300 g (10 oz) granulated sugar
2 tablespoons ground cinnamon,
  plus extra for dusting
2 tablespoons orange
  blossom water
250 g (8 oz) filo pastry
50 g (2 oz) butter, melted
1 egg yolk mixed with
  1 tablespoon water, to glaze
icing sugar, for dusting

- Line a baking sheet with greaseproof paper. Put the almonds, sugar, cinnamon and orange blossom water into a food processor and blend to a thick paste. Place the filo sheets under a clean, damp tea towel to prevent them drying out.

- Brush the top filo sheet with a little melted butter. Roll lumps of the almond paste into fingers, then place end to end in a line inside one edge of the pastry. Tucking in the ends to enclose the filling, roll up to form a long roll about a thumb's-width thick. Place in the centre of the prepared baking sheet, crease the roll like an accordion, then shape it into a coil. Repeat with the remaining sheets of filo, wrapping them tightly around the first coil.

- Brush the egg wash over the coil. Place in a preheated oven, 200°C (400°F), Gas Mark 6, for 20 minutes until lightly golden. Dust with icing sugar and a swirl of cinnamon. Serve warm or at room temperature.

1 Toasted Almond and Cinnamon Fingers

Mix together 175 g (6 oz) ground almonds, 3 tablespoons granulated sugar and 1 tablespoon ground cinnamon in a bowl. Add 1 tablespoon softened butter or ghee and work to a paste. Lightly toast 2–3 slices of brown or white bread, crusts removed and cut into fingers, on one side under a preheated grill. Turn them over, smear with the almond paste and toast for 2 minutes. Serve as a hot snack.

2 Almond Filo Fingers

Mix together 175 g (6 oz) ground almonds, 75 g (3 oz) granulated sugar, the grated rind of 1 lemon and 1 tablespoon softened butter. Cut 150 g (5 oz) filo pastry into rectangular strips and place under a clean, damp tea towel to prevent them drying out. Brush a little melted butter over a filo strip, then put 1 heaped teaspoon of the almond mixture at one end, fold over the long sides and roll up into a small cigar shape. Place on a lightly oiled baking sheet. Repeat with the remaining ingredients to make 16–20 fingers. Bake in a preheated oven, 200°C (400°F), Gas Mark 6, for 10–12 minutes. Dust with icing sugar and serve warm.

30 Almond and Toasted Sesame Seed Milk Pudding

Serves 4

120 g (4 oz) blanched almonds
1 litre (1¾ pints) milk
4 tablespoons rice flour
4 tablespoons water
100 g (3½ oz) granulated sugar
1–2 tablespoons sesame seeds
a few drops of almond extract

- Place the almonds in a food processor and whizz until finely ground. Set aside. Heat the milk in a heavy-based saucepan to boiling point. Mix the rice flour with the measurement water in a small bowl to form a smooth, thick paste. Take the milk off the heat and stir 2 tablespoons of the hot milk into the rice flour paste, then tip the mixture back into the milk, stirring continuously to prevent any lumps forming.

- Return to the heat and cook gently, stirring continuously, for about 5 minutes until the mixture begins to thicken. Add the ground almonds and sugar and cook gently for a further 15–20 minutes, stirring occasionally, until thick. Meanwhile, dry-fry the sesame seeds in a small, heavy-based frying pan over a medium heat for 1–2 minutes until they emit a nutty aroma.

- Stir the almond extract into the milk pudding, then pour into 4 serving bowls and scatter over the toasted seeds. Serve hot or chilled.

---

1 Almond and Sesame Seed Snaps

Dry-fry 225 g (7½ oz) chopped blanched almonds over a medium heat for 2–3 minutes. Tip into a bowl. Add 225 g (7½ oz) sesame seeds to the pan and dry-fry for 1–2 minutes. Add to the almonds. Place 125 ml (4 fl oz) honey and 120 g (4 oz) granulated sugar in a saucepan, bring to the boil and boil for 2 minutes, stirring continuously. Remove from the heat and stir in the almonds and seeds, then spread on an oiled baking sheet. Leave to cool, then loosen around the edges and break into pieces.

2 Almond and Sesame Seed Balls

Place 225 g (7½ oz) plain flour and 120 g (4 oz) wholewheat flour a heavy-based frying pan over a medium heat and stir continuously for 3–4 minutes until light brown and toasted. Tip into a bowl and stir in 120 g (4 oz) sifted icing sugar and 2 teaspoons ground cinnamon. Dry-fry 225 g (7½ oz) blanched almonds for 2–3 minutes until golden brown and remove, then dry-fry 225 g (7½ oz) sesame seeds for 1–2 minutes until they emit a nutty aroma. Tip both into a food processor and whizz until finely ground, then add to the flour. Mix together 120 g (4 oz) melted butter and 2 tablespoons runny honey, then combine with the flour and nuts. Roll small pieces of the mixture into cherry-sized balls, then roll in icing sugar. Press a slivered blanched almond into each one and serve with coffee or tea.

MOR-SWEE-HUD

30 Saffron Pears with Honey and Lavender

Serves 4

300 ml (½ pint) water
juice of 1 lemon
3–4 tablespoons honey
1 cinnamon stick
pinch of saffron threads
2–3 dried lavender heads,
  plus extra to decorate
4 firm pears with the stalks
  intact, peeled

- Place the measurement water and lemon juice in a heavy-based saucepan and bring to the boil. Stir in the honey, cinnamon stick, saffron threads and lavender heads and cook gently for 5 minutes.

- Add the pears and bring to the boil, then reduce the heat and cook gently for 20 minutes, turning and basting frequently. Serve hot with the cooking liquid drizzled over, decorated with a few lavender petals.

 Saffron, Pear and Lavender Tisane Place 4 tall, heatproof glasses on a tray and pour 1 tablespoon boiling water into each. Scatter 3–4 saffron threads into each glass and leave to steep for 2–3 minutes. Add 1 ready-to-eat dried pear and 1 lavender stem to each glass. Top up with boiling water, drizzle in 1–2 teaspoons runny honey to taste and serve as a digestive drink at the end of a meal, or as a pick-me-up drink at any time of day.

 Ice Cream with Saffron Syrup and Lavender Place 450 g (14½ oz) granulated sugar, 225 ml (7½ fl oz) water and a pinch of saffron threads into a heavy-based saucepan. Leave to steep for 5 minutes, then bring to the boil, stirring continuously until the sugar has dissolved. Reduce the heat and simmer for 10–12 minutes until the syrup coats the back of a wooden spoon. Spoon over vanilla ice cream and serve sprinkled with a few lavender petals. (The cooled syrup can also be strained into a sterilized bottle or jar, sealed and stored in the refrigerator for 3–4 weeks.)

MOR-SWEE-BAP

30 Grapefruit and Pomegranate Salad with Mint Yogurt

Serves 4

2 ruby grapefruit
2 white grapefruit
2 ripe pomegranates, quartered
2 tablespoons orange
    blossom water

For the yogurt

300 ml (½ pint) thick natural
    yogurt
small bunch of mint leaves,
    finely chopped, plus a few
    leaves to decorate
2 tablespoons runny honey

- Tip the yogurt into a bowl, fold in the mint and swirl in the honey. Cover and chill in the refrigerator.

- Using a sharp knife, remove the peel and pith from the grapefruit. Holding the grapefruit over a bowl to catch the juice, cut down between the membranes and remove the segments, then place in a serving dish.

- Holding the pomegranate quarters over a plate to catch the juice, bend each quarter backwards and flick the seeds into a bowl, leaving behind the white membrane and pith. Reserve 1 tablespoon of the seeds for decoration and scatter the rest over the grapefruit segments.

- Pour any grapefruit or pomegranate juice over the fruit with the orange blossom water and chill for 10–15 minutes in the freezer.

- Sprinkle the fruit with the reserved pomegranate seeds and mint leaves. Serve with the yogurt.

 Pomegranate and Orange Juice

Remove the seeds from 2 pomegranates as above, place in a food processor with 150 ml (¼ pint) water and whizz to a purée. Add 2–3 drops of red food colouring. Pass through a sieve into a jug, then stir in the juice of 2 oranges and 2 tablespoons orange blossom water. Add sugar to taste, pour into 4 glasses and decorate with a few mint leaves.

 Pomegranate Syrup Tea

Cut 4–5 pomegranates in half horizontally and press on a lemon juicer to extract the juice. Place about 300 ml (½ pint) of the juice and 350 g (11½ oz) granulated sugar in a heavy-based saucepan and bring to the boil, stirring continuously until the sugar has dissolved. Reduce the heat and simmer for 10 minutes. Add 2 drops of red food colouring and simmer for a further 2–3 minutes. To serve hot, spoon a little of the syrup into 4 heatproof cups, and top up with boiling water. To serve cold, pour a little of the syrup over some ice cubes in a glass and top up with cold water. (The cooled syrup can also be strained into a sterilized bottle or jar, sealed and stored in the refrigerator for 3–4 weeks.)

MOR-SWEE-CAY

 # Dates with Rosewater and Milk

Serves 4

225 g (7½ oz) ready-to-eat
pitted dates
75 ml (3 fl oz) rosewater
125 ml (4 fl oz) chilled milk
rose petals, to decorate

- Place the dates in a shallow bowl, pour over 2–3 tablespoons of the rosewater, cover and chill for 10–15 minutes.

- Drain the dates and pat dry with kitchen paper, then place in a serving dish. Put the remaining rosewater and the milk into separate small glass or china bowls.

- Arrange the dates, rosewater and milk on a tray and decorate with rose petals. To eat, first dip a date in the rosewater, then into the milk. Serve with tea.

 Date Syrup and Rosewater Sesame Paste Place about 350 g (11½ oz) creamed sesame paste (tahini) in a bowl and beat until smooth. Add 4 tablespoons date syrup and mix well, then drizzle over 1 tablespoon rosewater. Serve for breakfast with chunks of crusty bread for dipping, or spoon over toasted flatbreads and pancakes.

 Stuffed Date and Rosewater Fudge Place 450 g (14½ oz) ready-to-eat pitted dates on a work surface and place a walnut half into each opening, then pack closely in a lightly greased, shallow baking dish. Melt 225 g (7½ oz) butter in a saucepan, add 2 tablespoons granulated sugar and 2 tablespoons honey and stir continuously for 2–3 minutes until the sugar has dissolved. Beat in 250 g (8 oz) plain flour and stir over a low heat for 5–6 minutes until the mixture begins to turn golden brown. Beat in 2 tablespoons rosewater, then pour the mixture all over the dates, filling in any gaps, and leave to set for 15–20 minutes. Cut into small squares, dust with icing sugar and serve with coffee or tea.

MOR-SWEE-SEW

3 Strained Yogurt with Honeycomb

Serves 4

900 g (2 lb) thick natural yogurt
225 g (7½ oz) fresh honeycomb
ground cinnamon, for dusting

- Line a sieve with a large piece of muslin so that the edges flop over the sides, then place over a bowl. Tip the yogurt into the muslin and leave to drip for 25 minutes. Tip the strained yogurt into a bowl and beat until smooth and creamy.

- Spoon the yogurt into 4 serving bowls. Divide the honeycomb between the bowls and drizzle any loose honey over the top. Dust with cinnamon and serve immediately.

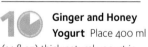 **Ginger and Honey Yogurt** Place 400 ml (14 fl oz) thick natural yogurt in a bowl. Peel and chop 25g (1 oz) fresh root ginger and, in batches, squeeze through a garlic press to extract the juice, holding the press over the yogurt. Beat the juice into the yogurt and swirl in 2 tablespoons runny honey. Serve for breakfast or as a snack.

 Spiced Honey Yogurt Place 5–6 tablespoons honey, the juice of 1 lemon, 2 cinnamon sticks, 1 teaspoon cardamom seeds, 2 star anise and 5–6 peppercorns in a heavy-based saucepan and bring to the boil, then reduce the heat and simmer gently for 5 minutes. Leave to cool in the pan to let the flavours mingle. Spoon 2–3 tablespoons thick natural yogurt into each of 4 serving bowls. Pass the honey mixture through a sieve and pour over the yogurt. Serve for breakfast or as a snack.

MOR-SWEE-NIQ

3⏲ Chilled Almond Milk

Serves 4

250 g (8 oz) blanched almonds
600 ml (1 pint) water
100 g (3½ oz) granulated sugar
1 tablespoon orange blossom
   water
ice cubes, to serve

- Place the almonds in a food processor and blend to a smooth paste, adding a splash of water to loosen.

- Place the measurement water and sugar in a heavy-based saucepan and bring to the boil, stirring continuously until the sugar has dissolved. Stir in the almond paste and simmer for 5 minutes. Stir in the orange blossom water and turn off the heat.

- Leave to cool in the pan to let the flavours mingle, then pass through a muslin cloth into a jug and squeeze tightly to extract all the milky liquid from the almonds.

- Pour into 4 glasses, add some ice cubes to each and serve immediately. Alternatively, chill the glasses in the refrigerator or freezer.

1⏲ **Chilled Yogurt Drink** Beat 450 g (14½ oz) chilled thick natural yogurt in a bowl until smooth. Gradually pour in 450 ml (¾ pint) chilled water, beating continuously, then add salt to taste. Put a few ice cubes into 4 glasses and pour over the yogurt. Scatter a little dried mint over each one and serve with spicy food.

 2⏲ **Chilled Vanilla Milk** Place 600 ml (1 pint) milk and 2 vanilla pods into a heavy-based saucepan and bring to just below boiling point. Turn off the heat, stir in sugar to taste and leave to cool. Remove the vanilla pods, slit open lengthways and scrape out the seeds. Strain the milk into a jug, stir in the seeds and pour into 4 glasses over ice cubes.

Alternatively, chill in the refrigerator before serving.

MOR-SWEE-SIR

 # Moroccan Mint Tea with Lemon Verbena

Serves 4

2 teaspoons Chinese Gunpowder
   green tea leaves
2–3 sugar lumps, plus extra
   to taste
large bunch of peppermint and
   garden mint leaves and stems
small bunch of lemon verbena
   leaves and stems

- Place the green tea and sugar lumps in a teapot. Pour over a little boiling water and leave to steep for 5 minutes.

- Stuff the mint and lemon verbena leaves into the pot, packing them in as tightly as you can. Add more sugar lumps to taste – the sugar enhances the flavour of the mint – and top up the pot with boiling water.

- Place the teapot over a pan of boiling water or over a low heat on the hob, or simply cover with a tea cosy. Leave the tea to brew for 10 minutes.

- Place 4 tea glasses on a tray. Pour some of the tea into a glass, then tip it back into the pot. Hold the pot high above the glasses and pour slowly so that bubbles form on top of the tea. Serve immediately.

 ### Quick Peppermint Tea

Trim several stems of peppermint to the size of your tea glasses. Place 1–2 leafy stems into each of 4 glasses with 1–2 sugar cubes or 1–2 teaspoons runny honey to taste. Fill each glass with boiling water, cover with a clean tea towel and leave to steep for 2–3 minutes. Serve hot.

 ### Iced Orange Mint Tea

Using a pestle and mortar, bruise a large bunch of peppermint, spearmint and garden mint leaves with 2 tablespoons granulated sugar. Add the sliced rind of 1 orange and bruise with the mint to release the flavours. Tip the orange and mint mixture into a heavy-based saucepan, add 2 tablespoons green tea leaves, 2–4 tablespoons granulated sugar and 600 ml (1 pint) water and bring to the boil, stirring continuously until the sugar has dissolved. Reduce the heat and simmer for 2–3 minutes. Stir in the juice of 2 oranges and the juice of 1 lime. Leave to cool in the pan. Strain into a jug and chill in the freezer for 10–15 minutes. To serve, fill 4 tall glasses with crushed ice, pour in the chilled tea and decorate with a slice of orange and a slice of lime.

 # Hot Spicy Tea with Chillies

Serves 4

2 cinnamon sticks

25 g (1 oz) fresh root ginger, peeled and finely sliced

6 cloves

4 dried red chillies

600 ml (1 pint) water

2–3 tablespoons honey

1 lemon, cut into 4 thick slices

- Place the spices and the measurement water in a medium saucepan and bring to the boil. Reduce the heat and cook gently for 15 minutes. Stir in the honey and simmer for a further 3–4 minutes.

- Strain the tea into 4 heatproof glasses, add 1 of the chillies to each and serve with a slice of lemon to squeeze over.

 ### Quick Ginger and Chilli Tea

Place 4 thick slices of peeled fresh root ginger, 4 dried red chillies and 400 ml (14 fl oz) boiling water in a saucepan and boil gently for 8–10 minutes. Strain the tea into 4 heatproof glasses, add 1 of the chillies to each and sweeten with honey to taste.

 ### Spiced Ras el Hanout Milky Tea

Place 300 ml (½ pint) milk, 2 cinnamon sticks, 4 thick slices of peeled fresh root ginger and 2 star anise in a saucepan and bring to just below boiling point. Stir in 1–2 teaspoons ras el hanout. Turn off the heat and leave to steep for 10–15 minutes. Meanwhile, put 1 tablespoon black tea leaves into a heatproof bowl, pour in 300 ml (½ pint) boiling water and leave to steep for 10 minutes. Pour the tea into the milk and bring to just below boiling point. Stir in 2–4 tablespoons honey to taste, then reduce the heat and simmer for 10 minutes. Strain the tea into a teapot and serve immediately in heated teacups.

Moroccan Coffee with Cardamom

Serves 4

4 coffee cups of water, about 100 ml (3½ fl oz) each
4 cardamom pods
4 teaspoons very finely ground Arabica coffee
4 teaspoons sugar

- Place the measurement water and cardamom pods in a small saucepan and carefully spoon the coffee and sugar on top. Gently stir the sugar and coffee into the surface of the water, making sure you don't touch the bottom of the pan with the spoon.

- Bring to just below boiling point over a medium heat, gradually drawing in the outer edges of the coffee into the middle to create a froth. Just as the coffee is about to bubble, spoon some of the froth into 4 coffee cups and pour in the coffee. Leave to stand for 1 minute before drinking to let the coffee grains settle at the bottom of the cups.

 Milky Cinnamon Coffee

Place 2 tablespoons finely ground coffee, 4 cinnamon sticks and 400 ml (14 fl oz) water in a saucepan and bring to the boil, stirring continuously, then turn off the heat and leave to steep for 10 minutes. Strain the coffee, reserving the cinnamon sticks. Pour back into the pan and heat gently to just below boiling point. Put 250 g (8 oz) condensed milk into a separate pan and heat gently to just below boiling point. Place the reserved cinnamon sticks into 4 cups, mugs or heatproof glasses. Pour in the coffee to just over halfway, then pour in the condensed milk. Dust the tops with ground cinnamon and serve immediately.

 Iced Cardamom and Cinnamon

Coffee Put 2 tablespoons finely ground coffee, 4 cinnamon sticks, 8 cardamom pods and 225 ml (7½ fl oz) water into a saucepan and bring to just below boiling point. Turn off the heat and leave to cool. Meanwhile, in a separate pan, heat 225 ml (7½ fl oz) water and 225 g (7½ oz) granulated, soft brown or muscovado sugar, stirring continuously until the sugar has dissolved. Boil for 2–3 minutes, then reduce the heat and simmer for 5 minutes. Stir in the coffee and leave to cool. Strain into a jug, reserving the cinnamon sticks and cardamom pods, and chill in the freezer for 10–15 minutes. Put the reserved cardamom pods and cinnamon sticks into 4 tall glasses, fill them with crushed ice and pour over the chilled coffee. Serve at once.

Index

Page references in *italics*
indicate photographs

Acknowledgements

Recipes by **Ghillie Basan**
Executive Editor **Eleanor Maxfield**
Senior Editor **Leanne Bryan**
Copy Editor **Jo Murray**
Art Direction **Tracy Killick and Geoff Fennell for Tracy Killick Art Direction and Design**
Original design concept **www.gradedesign.com**
Designer **Tracy Killick and Geoff Fennell for Tracy Killick Art Direction and Design**
Photographer **Will Heap**
Home Economist **Sunil Vijayakar**
Prop Stylist **Liz Hippisley**
Production **Allison Gonsalves**